MW01234509

This Earthly Tent
Me, God and MS

Janelle Green

This Earthly Tent
Me, God and MS
by Janelle Green

Printed in the United States of America

ISBN 978-1-60791-154-8

www.xulonpress.com

Acknowledgment

My Dear Friends,

Writing this book would have been impossible for me. With the writing skills of my childhood friend, Mary Anne Allread, these pages have come to print.

I could never thank Mary Anne enough for her tireless efforts over the last several years. She is a true close personal friend in every way. What an awesome friend to dig into my life.

God bless you greatly, Mary Anne.

Love, Janelle

I want to tell my story, and I want it to be written down, documented, so that my children, and the people I love, will be able to see how I live and what happens to me each day. One day, my children will wonder things about me and what I do during the day. I would like for them to be able to read about my life. Also, I might like to read it myself.

Nobody knows-nobody knows what happens to me. I sit in this wheelchair all day. People might think they know what happens to me, but they don't know. They don't know what all I encounter from the time I get out of bed in the morning till I go to bed at night. You know how you sometimes wish you could have your Mother back and talk to her and ask her things you never asked her when she was alive. Well, I know it is going to be that way with my kids when I am gone. I would like for them to be able to have my story documented somewhere so they can read it and maybe have some of their questions answered.

My name is Janelle. As a little child, I grew up in the country. In the summer I loved to walk in the sand barefoot doing all the typical childhood things. I used to go with my Daddy following rabbit trails. You see, he was a big rabbit hunter. As I got older, rabbit trails no longer appealed to me. By the time I became a teenager, living in the country no longer appealed to me either. I remember one day I had been out in the garden picking peas. As I was walking back to my house, I remember thinking to myself, that when I grow up, I will never live in the country. Ironically, the exact spot where I was standing when I had that thought is where the house I live in today stands. You never know which direction your life is going to take.

My parents, Lizzie and Gene Glenn, were good and hard working people. They both worked in cotton mills. In addition, my Daddy farmed his land. We attended Congaree Baptist Church where my Dad was a Deacon.

He died December 4th, 1963 when I was only 17 years old. He died of lung cancer. He smoked early in his life, then quit for ten years, then started again. That was a sad time.

4

In 1964, I graduated from high school and began working at the telephone company. One day, I was picking up a friend who rode to work with me, and a young man who lived across the street from her saw me. She told me later that he wanted to meet me. Reluctantly, I agreed to have dinner at her house to meet him. I never dreamed that I would go out with a man with red hair. He asked me out and I went because I didn't want to hurt his feelings. I was quiet and shy and not very worldly. Rick Green was outgoing and sure of himself. When he took me out, I saw that he could talk to anyone. He never met a stranger. I fell for him because he had something I didn't -the gift of gab. He still has that special talent today. He won me over with his outgoing personality and after a whirlwind six week relationship, we got married December 4, 1964. I was 18. He was almost 20. How young we were. Now that I am a mother, I certainly am glad that my children didn't jump into a marriage at such a young age and so quickly. Never did I realize that God was right there in the picture putting us together even so young. Looking back to the very beginning when Rick and I met, God had a plan even then, knowing that down the road we would spend many years together, married and raising three wonderful children.

Through those young years, we had a happy marriage. Our first child, Alan, was born in 1968. He was a beautiful baby with a reddish tint in his hair like his Daddy. We were living in Augusta, Georgia at the time and I loved being a Mom for the first time. When I was pregnant, Rick and I started going back to church regularly. We decided that it was important for us to give our children the same spiritual opportunities that we had been given.

Scott, our second son, was born in 1971. We were thrilled with our two little boys. We had moved back to West Columbia for Rick's job and bought a house overlooking the city on Starmount Drive. We stayed busy working and taking care of our little family.

In 1973, Rick and I were both involved in the Jaycees and Jaycee-ettes civic groups. Our groups were working on a project sending baby formula to the nuns at an orphanage in Vietnam.

Through this project, we started hearing about how these Vietnamese babies were being adopted out to different areas of the world. I started thinking, humm…I wonder if we could adopt. My thoughts were, we know how to have little boys. We have two. But we don't know how to have a little girl and we would like to have one. So we had a family meeting and let Alan and Scott help us decide. Our whole family decided to adopt a baby girl. We even had a family project. The children and Rick and I composed a booklet of drawings and the story of our little girl's adoption. I think the title was <u>One, Two, Then Three</u>. We began to fill out all the forms, had different agencies visit our home, and answered questions. We had to go through the South Carolina Children's Bureau to be approved. The process seemed so long, but in reality, it only took us about two years from the beginning to the day our daughter flew in from Saigon, now called Ho Chi Men City. We called her Leah. She was one month old when she was chosen for us and four months old when she came to us in 1975. Now our family was complete.

By this time, my Mother, Lizzie, had remarried. She had been single for about twelve years and was not happy with her lonely life. She told me that some evenings she would come home from work so tired. She would have a bowl of ice cream and fall asleep with her head on the kitchen table. She had to work so hard and was so lonely. So I was happy for her when she married Tyson Shumpert. He was a wonderful companion for her. She eventually retired from the mill after working there for 42 years.

So there I was, a young wife and mother, busy with my family and living an ordinary life. Little did I know that God had plans for me that would mean I would be facing many difficulties ahead.

I will continue my story with something that happened on a January morning in 1977, when my life took a different turn than I had expected. Here are notes from my journal written in my own hand.

January, 1977

I woke up at 5AM on January 24 and was numb in my right arm from my fingertips to my elbow. Over the next four to five days, I went numb completely from my neck to my toes. I went to see my doctor and he told me I had injured a nerve over my elbow. He said I had slept wrong on it or hit it. I knew I had not. He even said it might be "hysteria." On January 31, I was finally sent to a neurologist. He treated me like I was wasting his time, and told me that everything was normal. He took my sister in another room, and asked her what was bothering me. My sister tried to convince him that I had no problems, but he didn't seem to want to hear it. By this time, I was not only numb, I also was unable to do things for myself. I couldn't button my own buttons, tie my shoelaces, zip zippers. It got to the point that I could barely eat by myself. I could still bathe myself, but they were very jerky baths and I constantly dropped the soap and washcloth.

February 13, 1977

I woke up this morning and couldn't swallow. My throat was swollen practically shut. I went to the emergency room, and the doctor prescribed medication. At this point, I was sicker than I had ever been in my life. I even let my mother make milkshakes from raw eggs and I drank them freely, because I needed the strength they could give me so badly.

February 19, 1977

Feelings have left my legs again.

February 24, 1977

Some of the feeling started to come back in my hands.

March 11, 1977

Today I came down with a kidney infection.

March 12, 1977

Along with the kidney infection, I have lost feeling on the left side of my chest.

March 13, 1977

My back and left side are terribly numb.

March 23, 1977

Now the feeling is back in my back and trying to come back in my chest.

March 27, 1977

I now have feeling back in my chest.

April 11, 1977

Now my arms and hands are much better.

There are no journal entries from April, 1977 until May, 1978-over a year later. I was diagnosed with Multiple Sclerosis in 1977. I had experienced bouts of numbness at other times earlier in my life. I remember when Rick and I lived in North Augusta numbness occurred for no apparent reason. Also I had a problem with double vision when I was 15 years old. That is an early symptom of MS. In fact, that history of double vision at age 15 was one of the things that helped confirm a final diagnosis of MS. But it was not until that morning in January 1977 when I knew something was really wrong.

May, 1978

About 3 weeks before the end of school, I started having difficulty talking. The first few days only I could tell. I knew the words were not coming out like I was trying to say them. By that second week my speech was bad news. The words just would not come through my lips in the same manner they were passing through my brain. It wasn't long drawn out words as sometimes happens. The words were just mixed up or not coming out at all. At the end of three weeks this difficulty went away completely.

November 21, 1978

I woke up this morning to numb lips, just on the right side of my mouth. Then when I took my first drink I found that my tongue was numb on the right side. Also, in washing my face, I found the right side of my face numb. It was weird, like having Novocain.

November 22, 1978

The numbness moved down into my throat. It feels like I have a small piece of meat hung in my throat. I can't feel it until I swallow, but you swallow quite often, and not just at mealtime. I can remember having this same feeling about four years ago in my throat, although not the facial numbness. After seeing an ear, nose and throat specialist, and being told there was nothing in my throat, it eventually went away. I can't remember how long it took. In addition to this problem, there has been an added degree of fatigue, which I really don't need. During all this I have developed a terrible cold. Now to have a common cold when you have MS is almost like having the flu. My fatigue is so much worse.

November 28, 1978

Back in July of 1978, I had a Pap Smear, which came back abnormal. You just always assume they will be okay. Well this one came back showing a #3. A#5 indicates cancer. So this meant I had a condition that could turn into cancer. My doctor sent me to another doctor to have a colposcopy done. This was a procedure to look closely at the area with something like binoculars. Then I went back to my doctor to have cryosurgery (freezing the area with gases.) Two months later, I had another Pap Smear, and eleven days later it also came back a #3. That morning when the nurse called, I spent an hour in hell. I cried to the Lord until I couldn't breathe. I kept finding myself in the fetal position. Already, I had been through so much that I just couldn't believe it was happening again. I struggled with God for that hour and then a quiet peace come over me. I had fought for that hour, and now I finally realized that God was the winner, no matter how hard I fought. Even through that hour of struggle, I was saying "God, I know this is your plan, and it's perfect. It's just that right now I can't see straight." Boy, did I need His strength that morning. It was really a scene like nothing I had experienced before-not even when I was told that I had MS. It is amazing how God can give you so much strength when you are weakest. I can remember as a teen-ager thinking that if anything ever happened to my body that I would die. Well, here I am today with this very unhealthy body, and each day is an adventure. Not that I like the absence of my health, but to know that God not only walks beside me through each struggle, but He actually carries me most of the way.

December 8, 1978

Today I experienced extreme dizziness and lack of coordination. I drove, but should not have.

December 9, 1978

I came down this afternoon with sensitivity to light. I even had to wear sunglasses in the house. Later, at night, I had dull, frequent pains in my left eye. This lasted about two hours, and then the pain went away as quickly as it came.

December 10, 1978

I rode in the car on Sunday, and realized there was no way I could drive a car. It was like everything rushing at me, the road, trees, other cars, etc.

December 11, 1978

I think I am feeling pretty sorry for myself with all the complications of MS. Rick and I had made plans to join a share group, which begins this Thursday night. Judy Dominick, one of the group members, called and I told her that I had not talked it over with Rick, but with all the complications I had that I felt like we should not join their share group. Then she began to tell me about the book the group would be studying. It is called God Can Make it Happen. It is about optimistic attitudes and keeping your head up and expecting the most from God. Well, I realized this was exactly what I needed. So I changed my mind and said I would be there Thursday night.

December 12, 1978

A neighbor called and asked if I was going out today. I told her that I was having a problem and couldn't drive. I offered her my car. She wouldn't take the car unless I went with her. So I went and found I got sick to my stomach from the feeling that everything was coming at me.

December 13, 1978

This morning, I woke up just knowing my vision was going to be better. Well, as it turned out, my vision was worse today. This is the first time I have had any big problems with my eyes in 16 years. That was my original attack at the age of 15, in 1962. I came down with an infection of the optic nerve, which resulted in double vision. That was my only problem at that time and it lasted for months. My father put a patch over one lens of my glasses and that eliminated the double vision. Of course, I saw the doctor about every other day for a long time, then twice a week, and so on. I thank God for 16 years of sight.

I have a weird feeling in my nose and upper lip. It's not a numb feeling, but feels more like skin feels after putting Ben-Gay on it-sort of cold and weird. I feel like I am breathing air-conditioned air.

December 14, 1978

We started in the new share group tonight. We were going around the room reading verses out of the Bible. I sat there and could actually see to read, for the first time in a week. I was so happy, and shared the experience with the group.

December 15, 1978

Today, I drove for the first time in a week. It was only down to the school and back. I'm glad I didn't get myself into traffic. Turning my head was difficult, and judging distances was hard.

December 17, 1978

In church this morning, I had to put on my sunglasses because the bright lights really hurt my sensitive eyes. I have a lot of dizziness if I'm up too much.

February 21, 1979

I am having a lot of dizziness. Rick was in Charleston and called me. He thought I had taken a nerve pill because my speech was so slow and sluggish.

February 26, 1979

My writing is horrible. I walk like a warped car. Everything seems a bit off, my walking, talking, everything.

March 1, 1979

Becky called on Thursday and wanted to put me on the prayer chain. I was reluctant. She said it was my pride. She put me on and by Saturday, I had my spark back in my eyes. Then on Sunday, I was even energetic by afternoon.

March 7, 1979

Today I feel slow and tired and like I'm not accomplishing much, but I'm still better than the last 2 weeks.

March 9, 1979

These two weeks of my last round were really strange. The grip in my hands was bad-especially my right hand, since I depend on it more. When blowing my hair dry, for instance, to keep from dropping the dryer to the floor without realizing it, I had to constantly be thinking of keeping a grip on the dryer. This usually comes naturally, without thinking, but not during this period. It is also difficult for me to hold onto a pencil. It just drops out of my hand without me realizing it.

March 20, 1979

I am so exhausted, and have been since the first of March. Instead of getting better, I get worse. I find that I just can't vacuum anymore. When I do vacuum one room, I am finished for the day. I've spent a lot of time this month feeling sorry for myself. I am not very confident in myself and need even more encouragement from others, especially Rick.

I was talking to a friend a week or so ago, and we were speaking of another friend who was experiencing some numbness. I expressed concern, and she said, "Oh, when you got sick, you had lots of other problems, too." I let her know quickly that numbness was my first real sign when I realized that I had a problem.

April 8, 1979

I started having numbness in my right foot tonight.

April 9, 1979

By this morning, I now have numbness in both feet.

April 11, 1979

I awoke with numbness up to my knees yesterday. As this day goes on, I feel less and less numbness in my feet, and my legs feel better too. Praise the Lord.

I have a special friend who prays for me all the time. She calls me when there is going to be a healing ministry in town. She gets others to pray for me and is convinced that I will be healed. I told her that in here (pointing to my head), I am healed. In II Corinthians 12:7, Paul says that he was given a thorn in the flesh. In verse 8, he says, "I entreated the Lord three times that it might depart from me." Oh how many times have I prayed to be healed. In verse 9, it says, "My Grace is sufficient for you, for power is perfected in weakness. Most gladly, therefore, I will rather boast about my weakness, that the power of Christ may dwell in me." Paul goes further in verse 10 to say, "When I am weak, yea, I am strong."

I have really learned to believe in the power of prayer in the past 27 months. Take my quick recovery from numbness this morning. My Circle was meeting this morning, and said they would pray for me. I know they did.

May 9, 1979

Today I started having problems walking.

May 11, 1979

The walking is really bad now. I can't point the left foot and can't make the foot go forward. My back seems to be off, and it feels like one leg is shorter than the other. It tires me out to walk.

I read an article recently which made me understand my bladder problem better. It said that sometimes the bladder does not release all the urine. This is exactly what is happening to me. Instead of the bladder frequency I thought I had, I go so frequently because I release such small amounts each time.

May 12, 1979

My walking is really bad now. It is exhausting just to walk across the room.

MS really does play havoc with a marriage. With this leg problem came marriage problems also. Rick loves me very much, but needs a place to vent his feelings.

May 13, 1979

I did not try to go to Sunday School or church today. I stayed home and rested this morning so that I could go to a special service we had at church tonight. Ben Haden was there. We had terrible storms and his private plane was held over in Greenwood, SC. Our minister was so good with all those people. There were Baptists, Methodists, Lutheran, everything. Our minister had us worshipping together as Christians and if Ben Haden had not been able to get there, I think everyone would have gone away happy after worshipping together

April 21, 1980

Over all I have been doing well this past year. I can no longer vacuum my house or do lots of other things. But, I am walking, talking clearly, and raising three children. If the Lord will just give me the opportunity to raise my children…

I am so determined that MS will not take away my ability to walk. I have marked off a course out from my driveway, down the street and back that is a mile long. I walk it every day to keep my leg muscles toned so that I will never have to be in a wheelchair. I am determined that MS will not beat me.

Yesterday in Sunday school, we talked about deeds by which we will be judged. It seems that deeds mean different things to different people. God gave us different personalities to use very differently in his work, and I feel our deeds are different. I might mop a floor for a friend who is not feeling well, or I might talk at length with a friend who has problems. To me these are deeds.

May 21, 1980

I started having shortness of breath and my heart is skipping beats. It got so bad I had to go and have an EKG and it was perfect. The Dr. gave me nerve pills and that took care of it. But, on Friday, I came home from Leah's end of the year picnic, went to bed at 12:30 and slept till 3:30. Then I went to bed at 9:00PM. Saturday, I slept all day long without stopping, except to get up for lunch and then again for supper. For 24 hours straight, I slept, and with no bladder problems, too.

May 27, 1980

Becky Jones and I were sitting on the deck in the early morning sun about 10 AM and I had a strange pulling sensation in my right eye. I commented to Becky about this. Later as the day passed my face started to change and looked liked someone who had had a stroke. The left side was paralyzed. When I smiled, it was only on the right side and sort of pulled from the left making my right cheek look extra big. I realized later that the pulling sensation in my right eye had only been from the fact that my left eye was not closing at all to close out the sun and that made the right feel an extra pull because of the lack of balance of the two. I went all week thinking this was just another MS experience. Then by Friday, Rick insisted I should see my neurologist. When I talked with him on the phone, he said I should come in because it could be either MS or Bells Palsy. After examining me thoroughly, he decided it probably was Bells Palsy especially since I had no numbness in my face.

May 30,1980

Our church family camp at the YMCA Camp Columbia started. We went last night for the evening activities. Then today, we went for the whole day really hoping I would not become overtired. Tonight, the children stayed at the camp with friends and Rick and I came home.

June 1, 1980

This morning I awoke at 6 AM to the sound of chirping birds, which wasn't really a pleasant sound because I wanted to sleep longer. Then I was so very wide awake I realized the Lord wanted me alert and awake to get up and read his Word and meditate on Him first thing that morning. This had been the whole concept of our retreat-Family Quiet Time. So I got up, started a pot of coffee, and tried to wake Rick. He got ugly about me waking him at 6:30 in the morning. When he's asleep, you simply don't interrupt him. But, in 5 minutes he was awake and in the kitchen reading James I. We really had a pleasant experience sharing God's word and praying together. Great! We got home from camp about 4PM. Sometime between 4 and 8 o'clock, my face went back to normal. "To God be the Glory." We were with so many Christian friends all week end and they had shared in my problem and prayed for me and I have NO doubt that God took immediate action and healed me. What a testimony God is planting in my mind. I called several friends and shared this immediately.

June 26, 1980

I started having vision problems today. As I was driving the children to swim lessons, I noticed a change in my ability to drive well because of my sight. Grannie Green, Rick's Grandmother, was here visiting.

June 27, 1980

I awoke and knew I would not be able to drive to swimming lessons and called my friend Vanda to drive. I ate breakfast and since Grannie was here and I was feeling so bad, I went back to bed and simply passed out. I can only remember Alan coming in a few times and asking if I was OK. I missed lunch. When Rick came home, he fried fish and insisted that I get up and eat. I took one bite and was sick on my stomach. I went back to bed. I started throwing up and threw up all night. Every sip I took of coke or whatever came back as 2 sips. I would go back to bed and have chills so bad Rick would have to wrap his body around me to warm me. This went on all night with only a little sleep. By 7 am it was still bad (dry heaves) and Rick took me straight to the emergency room. My doctor met me there. He saw I was having an exacerbation and was dehydrated. He immediately put me on an IV and started me on liquids. I was a very sick person. They started me on ACTH. I had never had any medication for MS before this. They found infection in my urinary tract. They started me on 80cc of ACTH. I complained that I could not stand it. So the Dr. cut it back to 40cc. I was given that for five days, then the vein where the IV was put went bad and they decided to just take me off ACTH. He took me off and put me on cortisone, which is still a steroid and makes me feel weird. I ate less during that week than ever before. It took till Thursday to get my appetite built up again. Friday morning I came home. So I was in the hospital from June 28th till July 3rd.

July 4, 1980

I got up this morning feeling good. For the first time, I had energy. On Friday when I came home I could hardly walk up the two steps to get in the door. Now one day later, I have walked a lot. As a matter of fact, my legs are terribly sore because I have not been used to walking for a week.

July 6, 1980

I did not sleep well last night and woke feeling miserable this morning. I went back to bed at 9:30 and didn't get up again until 11:30.

July 7, 1980

I called my neurologist this morning and he took me off the Prednisone. What a relief. Maybe I can start getting better now.

July 28, 1980

So far I have steadily improved, except for my energy. I have to work 5 minutes and lie down 10 minutes. This was really getting me down until yesterday when I realized I had written that very thing in my diary before. So now I'm on the upswing. I feel better about pulling out since I know with God's help I have pulled out before.

October 22, 1980

Praise the Lord! I haven't had anything of importance to write for three months. In James 5:11 it says..."The Lord is full of compassion and is Merciful." James 4:14,15 says..."You are just a vapor that appears for a little while and then vanishes away." You ought to say "If the Lord wills, we shall live and also do this so that." I never know from one day to the next, and neither do you.

November 4, 1980

My mother was operated on last week and it turned out to be cancer of the bladder. On Tuesday, the day of her surgery, I got up at 6 am and got to the hospital by 7:30, left the hospital at 4:30, went to vote and was back at the hospital from 7 till 9 pm. I visited her again on Wednesday and by Thursday I could see a difference in my vision and energy. By Friday, I was worse. I made plans to go this morning and do Mother's hair. Then this morning came, and I couldn't get out of bed. I started throwing up and was unable to keep anything on my stomach. By late afternoon I kept a saltine down and a little Coke.

November 5, 1980

Today I spent most of the day in bed, although I did get more food down.

November 6, 1980

I'm up and feeling a little peppier. My balance is terrible still. I ate a little breakfast.

November 8,1980

I woke up with the bed spinning. I began to throw up as soon as I stood up. By late afternoon, I had about stopped throwing up, but still couldn't eat.

November 10, 1980

I was able to keep some food down today.

November 11, 1980

I went in the hospital at 3 PM. It took all day to get a room. Rick took me and they brought a stretcher to the car and took me in and straight to my room. They started an IV then. I was a sick person. My body pulled to the left if I tried to walk and I would fall. I couldn't turn my head left or right without getting sick.

November 23, 1980

My head has been numb on the left side. My whole left side, even half of my tongue has been numb. I have been miserable. It lasted ten or twelve days. My tongue is still funny feeling.

November 30, 1980

I stopped using the walker and started holding onto furniture. My walking got worse. I could barely drag myself. Rick brought me a wheelchair from the MS Society. We both cried.

December 20, 1980

I feel as if I've been in a time bomb and lost one whole month. Yesterday I started walking with a cane for the first time. God is at work.

December 31, 1980

I drove to Spartanburg to take Grannie home.

January 1, 1981

Today I fixed New Year's Day dinner for Mother and Tyson.

January 2, 1981

I am not feeling well. I am beginning to not walk very well. My walking is getting bad. We went out with Vanda and Bob anyway to eat Chinese food and to a movie. Vanda had to walk me to the bathroom.

January 3, 1981

I stated throwing up again.

January 5, 1981

I was sick all weekend. I also walked with the walker all weekend. I am pulling to the left again.

January 30, 1981

I drove to West Columbia today for the first time. Before this I had only been able to drive in South Congaree. I had some confidence that I haven't had before.

February 4, 1981

Today I drove to downtown Columbia. I did nicely. My biggest accomplishment today was that I was able to sweep and mop my kitchen for the first time in three months.

October 28, 1981

If I look strong-let me tell you how weak I am. When I lose sight of where my strength comes from, I lose my strength. Lord, help me to keep sight of you. I've spent my morning having a pity party. Forgive me, please.

My Mother is in the hospital. They don't know what is wrong with her. This past weekend was my "Women to Women" retreat. God just slammed the door in my face. I certainly couldn't leave with Mother sick and in the hospital. Then, too, I had been having bladder problems for a week. So my decision was not to go. Then Friday, Scott got sick with a virus and was sick through Monday. I was needed at home. Now my body feels drawn and full of anxiety and tension. Help me, I pray. I don't want to have an attack. I believe, according to the Word of God, that "all things, whatever you shall ask in prayer, believing, you shall receive." Matthew 21:22. "Therefore, I say unto you, whatever things you desire, when you pray, believe that you receive them, and you shall have them." Mark 11:24. "And I say unto you, ask and it shall be given you; seek and you shall find, knock, and it shall be opened unto you. For everyone that asks receives, and he that seeks finds, and to him that knocks, it shall be opened." Luke 11:9,10. "And whatever you shall ask in My name, that will I do, that the Father may be glorified in the Son. If you shall ask anything in My name, I will do it." John 14: 13, 14.

May 26, 1982

I am on a leash. Tension, bladder problems, bad walking when tired, dizziness, FATIGUE. But, Praise the Lord, I'm ok.

August 30, 1983

Starting last week, I have had numbness in my right arm and hand. It hurts all through the night. School started August 25. I can only guess that the trauma of this is my problem. I now walk with a bad limp because of my right leg. The muscle that lets you point your toes and push your foot into a shoe is limp. When tired, my right leg gets like a rubber band.

August 31, 1983

Today I called about therapy.

September 5, 1983

My right leg is bad. I can't push my leg forward without dragging it. The numbness in my right arm and body is better. A week ago when I put deodorant under my right arm it was a strange feeling. That is better now.

September 6, 1983

I am exhausted. Just walking to the bedroom is exhausting.

September 7, 1983

I drag my right leg bad. Rick says I'm going to wear it out. It feels like my knee is going to bend backwards. It is tiring, but this is the day that the Lord hath made.

September 8, 1983

I started walking with a walker today. I would feel fine if walking didn't tire me out so.

September 9, 1983

About 9 PM tonight I got up and walked in the den and it was much improved. It's still not great but better.

September 10, 1983

As of this morning, I am back to where I was before last night. I'm just looking up.

September 11, 1983

I did not go to Sunday School because I couldn't climb the stairs. I drove to church and used my walker to get around. My energy level has remained high. I go and go and don't tire out. This is unusual for when I am experiencing a problem.

Sept 12, 1983

Betty took me to see Dr. Abbott this morning. I walked with a cane. I'm not walking good. By nighttime, I was walking pretty good and barely dragging my foot.

September 13, 1983

I am walking a little worse this morning. I feel nervous all over and have no energy.

September 14, 1983

I rested more today. I am walking with no help. Praise God. I have had two weeks of not walking well at all.

September 29, 1983

I am walking better, but if I'm tired I will still drag my right foot some. I'm just proud to be walking. Thank you God.

May 21, 1984

I still have the same limp in my right leg that began August 31, 1983. I have had it for nine months. But I am still proud to be walking.

My Mother, Lizzie, died July 2, 1984.

November 5, 1984

The limp in my right leg is worse. Lord, help me to see through it to you. Fatigue is bad and I'm very depressed. My house is ugly and nasty.

May 23, 1985

I still have the limp in my right leg, now worse than ever. Outside the house I'm usually using a cane. It gives me credibility anyway and people know I'm not drunk. I tire out easily and have to rest a lot. But, yesterday I went alone to Eckerd's and spent $39, then went to the shoe shop, the cloth shop, Jack Rabbit Photo and took Scott to Papa's to cut grass.

August 16, 1985

I can barely hold a pen or walk. I went outside this afternoon and it took thirty minutes to get back in crawling most of the way. Lord, I'm through and I want to go Home.

August 21, 1985

I woke up with my ears ringing. I thought it was caused by allergies. I took decongestants for two days and nothing cleared up.

August 23, 1985

I made an appointment with an ear specialist for Monday.

August 24, 1985

I woke up sick and throwing up. It continued all day. I couldn't keep anything on my stomach except four small bites of cantaloupe.

August 25, 1985

Today marks one week since calling in the elders and being anointed with oil and prayed for to be healed. August 18 was the date. This morning, I threw up first thing as I stepped out of bed. Rick called Dr. Abbott. He said that if I had not quit throwing up by 3pm he was going to put me in the hospital. Rick had my prescriptions filled for nausea and cortizone. He got me some cantaloupe, grapes, and honeydew melon. I slowly ate them and kept my eyes open. By 6:30 PM, I asked for a plate of real food.

August 26, 1985

My sister, Betty brought food for tonight. So did Linda Brooks.

August 27, 1985

Sylvia Drennon brought dinner for tonight.

August 28,1985

Martha Porter brought dinner for tonight.

August 29, 1985

Sylvia took me to the ear doctor today.

August 31,1985

I drove today for the first time. I'm still dizzy. My vision is super bad too. But I made it to Brendles and went inside too.

September 1, 1985

I couldn't go to morning church. Rosemary Fitts made Sunday lunch for my family. How nice that was.

September 2, 1985

My fatigue and hearing are still very bad.

September 18, 1985

My hearing is still bad in my left ear. I cannot hear on the telephone with that ear or if someone is sitting to my left, I can't hear them.

September 25, 1985

I was able to hear on the telephone in my left ear for the first time today. I was talking to my sister, Nev. Praise God. I am not back to normal but at least I can hear much better.

November 20, 1985

Sometime recently I started becoming numb in my right side. It's like an imaginary line is going through the center of me, and one side is numb and the other isn't. I felt like I was walking on a stick instead of a right leg.

November 27, 1985

Dr. Brannon put me on Prednisone and bed rest.

January 14, 1986

I am on my second exacerbation that I have had in three weeks time. Last Tuesday, January 7th I became numb on the left side of my body. Two weeks before it had been the right side. As soon as the right cleared up, the left went numb. I have no balance and have to hold on to furniture or use my walker. This past weekend my neck became very stiff and I couldn't turn my head. That is better now but is still stiff. I'm in bed most of the time.

January 16, 1986

Dr. Brannon started me on Prednisone again today. I am now numb on my left side. I had just gotten over being numb on my right side. For that I had taken Prednisone too. I've had double vision for 3 days. This left side has given me more all around problems than the right side did. I have to walk with my walker.

January 19, 1986

I can stay up only about 2 or 3 hours at a time. Rick says my eyes look better tonight. I still walk terrible. My vision is bad and my hearing is all messed up. I'm on prednisone again in different doses this time. I take 25 mg. at 8AM and 25 mg. at 8 PM now. Last time I just took 50 mg. in the morning.

January 21, 1986

Dr. Brannon put me in Richland Memorial Hospital. He said it was so he could put me on ACTH. Instead he left me on Prednisone. I haven't recovered at all. Everything seems worse. I even soiled my pants one morning while in route to the bathroom. I travel so slowly and have just lost control of that muscle.

January 29, 1986

I am no better. On Monday, I was ready to check myself into Ricard Nursing Home. Judith Simpson came to visit me that morning and stayed from 10AM till 1:30PM. We cried together, laughed together, and prayed together. It is nice to have friends like her.

I have difficulty breathing at times. It feels like I can't get a deep breath. I can hardly eat. Holding a glass is practically impossible. I have a lump in my throat and it is hard to swallow. I am now home from the hospital, but I am no better.

February 1, 1986

I am still no better. My dear friend, Rosemary Fitts, has stayed beside me, checking on me, keeping my child, cooking for me, praying, washing my hair, washing clothes, visiting me in the hospital. What a Christian! Also my sister, Betty, has been right there too. Such love!

February 5, 1986

Today was a good day.

February 6, 1986

This has been a bad day. I didn't sleep well last night. Rick went out of town today to Atlanta. Mary Lou Merchant stayed with me till 2:30 and Judith Simpson stayed in the afternoon.

February 7, 1986

Today would have been my Daddy's birthday. He would have been 74. Kaye Gardner came and stayed with me. Then Eleanor Hawk came for the afternoon. Alice Hygema came too. By afternoon, I was exhausted.

February 8, 1986

Leah and I were home alone today. I have better endurance. I have stood and washed dishes twice and walked a little without my walker in the kitchen. I am much better today. My walking is still like a toddler.

February 9, 1986

I felt good at 7 AM when I awoke. I went to church for the first time tonight. I used the Rascal. I was tired when I got home.

February 10, 1986

I am walking better today. Scott even noticed and told me last night that I was going to get better.

February 11, 1986

I'm still walking better, but not running any races though.

February 13, 1986

My share group is coming to my house tonight. I feel stronger.

February 14, 1986

I really feel good today. I took my bath early and did my hair. The nurse came and I still feel good. I stayed up 51/2 hours and then crashed.

February 21, 1986

I woke up at 5:30 AM feeling well. It's 8 AM now and I still feel well. My share group came here last night. Thank you, God.

February 24, 1986

I slept until 9 AM after going to bed at ten last night. I felt bad all day and stayed in bed a lot.

March 1, 1986

It is 9:30 at night and I haven't been back to bed all day, since 8 AM this morning. This is my longest day up in six weeks. I can't walk any better but I think my stamina has improved.

March 4, 1986

The left side of my lower lip is numb.

March 5, 1986

My left arm is numb again. So is my left knee. I sleep all the time. God help me. I got in the bathtub Tuesday night and could not get out. Rick had to get me out. I was completely helpless. I have no coordination at all now.

March 7, 1986

My chest is numb again. My legs are very stiff. I feel 80 years old. I only feel good in bed-asleep. I have no sense of coordination. I am sick of this. I have pus in my urine also. The urologist put me on a daily pill to fight the infection.

March 9, 1986

This was probably my worst day ever both physically and mentally.

March 11, 1986

I woke up yesterday feeling better than the day before. Today, I think my head is clearer. Mentally, I feel fine. I can't walk good or stand over eight minutes, but I feel good.

March 21, 1986

I scream out in anger almost every day. I can't walk, I can't bend, I fall all the time, I stoop and end up in the floor and then I can't get up. I have to crawl to where I'm going. This is no existence.

March 24, 1986

Sunday, I was not doing well. I forced myself to go the pre-Easter service Sunday night. I had such trouble getting ready. I couldn't put on my panty hose. My legs just wouldn't hold me up and I kept falling.

Tuesday morning Dr. Brannon called me and I told him how bad I was doing, including the loss of back muscles, leg muscles, everything, even bowels. Today I feel better so far. It's still morning. Dr. Brannon told me I could increase my lioresal to 4 times a day instead of three.

I never started increasing it, because I felt like the lioresal might be aggravating the problem.

March 26, 1986

I drove for the first time yesterday. Rick couldn't get home from golf in time to take Leah to dancing so I tried. I had to use hand controls and couldn't handle a lot of traffic.

March 25, 1986

Dot Langfitt visited with me today. I had been in the wheelchair 99% of the time for about 6 days. I had started tapering off on the Lioresal and by today I was able to walk again. Scott came home from school. I let him in the door and he said, "Mom, you're looking so much better and you're walking."

March 28, 1986

I went to see Dr. Brannon and told him of the improvement. He said the Lioresal would not have done this. I disagreed.

April 4, 1986

Betty went with me and Leah and I drove to Sheppard's Glass Company and had my car mirrors repaired. Mr. Sheppard prayed for me with Mark. I then drove to Dutch Square. We took my chair out and shopped all over. Then we went to Barrett's Shoes and I used my walker there. What a busy day, my busiest since January 1st. I had only driven once before Saturday a week ago. I drove to the meat market. I didn't get out though. Leah did.

April 5, 1986

Rick, Alan and Scott went to Spartangurg to see Grannie. Leah was at Carowinds with Nova. I decided to go shopping by myself at K-Mart with my chair.

April 6, 1986

Today I went to Sunday School for the second Sunday since January 1st.

April 7, 1986

Today I called Rosemary and Stephen and had them over for lunch.

April 8, 1986

I am sitting in the floor –Indian style-in front of the coffee table, eating lunch (my favorite way). I haven't been able to do this in three months. Thank You, God.

April 9, 1986

I feel bad today. It got cooler outside overnight. I don't know if that has anything to do with it or not.

April 12, 1986

I planned a shopping trip to get me some clothes today. I took Leah and Jill Brooks. We got gas and then lunch at a drive in window. Then we came home. A week ago, I was out shopping by myself. Now I am in bed.

April 13, 1986

I didn't go to church today, I'm too sick.

April 14, 1986

I'm sick, not nauseated, just weak and can't walk.

April 15, 1986

I'm filled with anger today. My emotions are running wild, anger, hate, unfairness, everything. I'm losing strength in my left leg starting today for the first time. The knee just gives away. I hate the whole mess.

April 21, 1986

I'm much better today. My left leg is stronger. I walked out and down into my garage last Saturday with no cane just holding on. I went out to the trash cans. That's coming a long way.

May 8, 1986

I feel great. Each week we can see improvement. This is really exciting. Thank you Lord. Love, Janelle.

May 26, 1986

I'm feeling great. Last week I went out every day-all day. This Monday morning I sort of paid the price. Thank you God. I still can't walk any better. I use my chair and Canadian canes.

June 4, 1986

I've been in the road for two weeks-having a ball. But now my right leg is numb and I have total fatigue. I hate this. But I stand with you, God.

June 6, 1986

We went to Alan's graduation-me in my Rascal. Alan had a graduation pool party tonight. Warren and Rose came yesterday.

June 7, 1986

Leah had an end of school party.

June 8,1986

I had to go to bed. I can't walk or go on. I have lost the strength in my good leg (my left one) now. Last week I showed Nova how I could lift my left leg straight to the ceiling and could hardly lift my right. As of now, I can no longer lift my left leg. I can barely drag my right. My left hand is weaker.

June 11, 1986

I am still the same. I'm in bed all the time.

June 17, 1986

After a week and two days in bed, I have come a long way. Last week I fell down every time I got up. One day I was in the house alone (Scott and Leah were swimming) and I fell. I was three feet from the telephone when it started ringing and I couldn't pull my body to it. My shoulder muscles were even weak. Now my knees aren't buckling out from under me. I can stand and brush my teeth and wash my face. Night before last I got in the tub and out by myself. Rick had been putting me in and out one leg at a time. He just about broke his back lifting me out. Four days ago I could barely bend my knees without falling down. I'm trying to stay in bed and be good.

July 5, 1986

At 7:30 PM tonight, I walked through my bedroom, then to the kid's bathroom. While there a thought went through my mind. I will walk again and walk perfect. I don't know if it was my thoughts, because for some reason I was walking as I had not in six or eight months. I was able to pick up my right foot and put it down. My hops seemed level instead of off kilter. I could lift my right foot and cross my legs. Wow! By Sunday morning I was back.

July 16, 1986

Yesterday I noticed my right leg had become numb. By Wednesday, I still felt bad but pushed on and went shopping. By afternoon, I was in bed.

July 17, 1986

I am in bed completely. I can't walk over a few feet. I am very fatigued.

July 18, 1986

I am still in bed all day and night.

July 20, 1986

Rudolph came and talked me into getting out of bed. I went out to the pool on my Rascal with my pajamas on. I am starting back uphill.

July 23, 1986

Jim Kirk called me tonight and wanted to share his testimony with me. He told me that the Lord had really laid a burden on him while he was praying in the Spirit. He assured me that I am one of

God's special people and that He is walking with me through all of this. The Lord speaks through so many unbelievable people.

October 21, 1986

Jesus, life if getting so hard. I can't deal with it any more. If I had the nerve, I'd do away with myself. This morning, I awoke at 6 AM and noticed my balance was worse than ever. Then at 7:30 I had to drive the children to school. (Lord, thank you for my children. They give me a reason to keep going.) While driving, my eyes went wild and I couldn't see and a wave of nausea went all through my body. I spent all day in bed, only eating a small bowl of broth. Help me, Lord.

October 25, 1986

Today I drove myself to the beauty shop for a perm. Thank You, God.

October 30, 1986

I had a mammogram today at 9:30 AM. I left the hospital at 10:30 and came home. I was sitting at my kitchen counter eating when the nurse called and said they found something in my right breast. She said I needed to come back and have an ultrasound to see if it is a cyst or a mass.

November 3, 1986

After waiting all weekend, I went for the ultrasound today. I have 4 or 5 cysts in my right breast. Dr. Bennett says we will do nothing about them at this time.

November 6, 1986

I felt bad today. I went to bed without a bath at 9:15 PM. That is not like me.

November 7, 1986

I stayed in bed all day and slept. My vision keeps going bonkers. I squint my eyes to keep the light out and can't turn my head too fast or my vision gets blurred and goes double.

November 8, 1986

I still felt sick today, but was well enough to go to church tonight. I did have to wear sunglasses to protect my eyes.

November 10, 1986

My eyes are better and so is everything else.

November 16, 1986

Lord, do you love me? Nobody else does. Rick just hollers at me when I'm down. Help me. I would take my life today if I wouldn't hurt my children. Help me, Lord.

December 4, 1986

I can hardly hold onto a pencil. It slides out. Last night for the first time spasms of my legs woke me up. I had to take Lioresal. This is bad. Walk with me Lord, I'm getting bad.

December 9, 1986

Yesterday I felt like I would be in a convalescent home within six months. Today I'm better. I can walk better and I can smile.

January 14, 1987

About four days ago, my left leg became spastic for the first time. This made me sad.

May 18, 1987

I haven't written in 4 months, not because I have been well, but I just got sick of writing about my many problems. For the past week I have really been down. I'm through fighting. I have no fight left. I would like to go to sleep and not wake up. I'm so tired. I feel fatigue like I have never had before. I can barely walk. Help me, God.

June 9, 1987

Until today I took ½ Lioresal for spasticity. Today I started taking a whole pill as the lesser dose did not stop the pulling and jerking.

December 15, 1987

Tonight I took 6 Lioresal pills in a four hour period. The pulling and jerking absolutely would not stop.

December 16, 1987

I found out I overdosed on Lioresal. After taking those 6 Lioresals last night, I slept till 1:30 PM today. I couldn't think straight. Leah stayed home sick with sinus problems today. She was able to fix meals for me and take care of me. I don't know what I would have done without her.

December 20, 1987

It took me three or four days to think straight again after taking too many Lioresals.

January 15, 1988

I had some pains in my head this afternoon behind my right ear.

January 16, 1988

I have had those pains behind my right ear all day and all night.

January 17, 1988

By 4:00 PM, the pain was unbearable and I had to call Dr. Brannon. I told him my problem and that I didn't know if I should have called him or my family doctor. He said this sounded like an MS problem. He said in some younger MS patients there are facial pains which vary somewhat from what I am describing. Mine is above and behind my right ear.

January 22, 1988

My whole right side is highly affected after those head pains. Writing is very hard now. Walking is practically impossible. My right leg goes completely out from under me. I'm losing my will to keep going.

October 20, 1988

My walking is worse than ever. I can only stand about one minute, sometimes only ten seconds or so.

April 8, 1993

I can't walk at all. Also, I have no balance. I can still get in the tub. I love my tub baths. My right leg will barely hold me up now. I have to lock my knee in. Even this won't last much longer.

Since January of this year, I can no longer go shopping on my own. I can't load my scooter in my car. I can't close the tailgate. I don't have the energy.

January 21, 1995

Over this past weekend, I lost a lot of strength in my right side.

October 20, 1995

Well-I drove my van for the last time today. Betty was cleaning my house today and I wanted to run errands. Betty had to literally pick me up and put me in my van. I drove to the Hess station and had Jane Sligh, who works there fill my van up with gas. She had been filling it for me for two years. I told Jane my driving was over. I left and cried badly as I drove away. I left there and went to the bank and drove through the drive-in window. Veronica, the window teller, waited on me as she had for years. I told her that I had MS and that I wouldn't be coming back any more. As I pulled away I was crying badly again. I left there and went to Gaddas and Dot Franklin's house and cried for an hour. It is a terrible feeling to lose the ability to drive and to lose the independence that goes along with it.

That heartbreaking entry of October 1995 was the last time I wrote in my journal in my own handwriting. I did get other people to write several other entries for me.

January 1, 2002

Sometime in the last 3 weeks, I lost the ability to write.

January, 2003

It is a year later. I can tell you that not being able to write is the biggest loss of all. It is even a bigger loss that not being able to walk.

August, 2003

Today I began to pass blood when I urinate. I have passed some blood prior, but not like yesterday and today.

August 31, 2003

Today I passed a kidney stone the size of a grapefruit seed. It was my first ever and was painful, but not excruciatingly so. I knew something was happening that was not ordinary.

Those were the last entries in my journal. In September 2003, I called my old friend, Mary Anne Allread, with a plan. That is when I decided that I wanted to write my whole story and put it into a book. She agreed to help me put my life story into print and we began working together for that purpose. We began to have regular visits to work on my book. It has been wonderful to rekindle our old friendship with these frequent visits.

Looking Back

Looking back over my journal entries for the past 25 years, I can see the pattern of the ups and downs of my disease. Multiple Sclerosis is that kind of illness. I was diagnosed in 1977 with Relapsing-Remitting MS, which is characterized by periods of flare-ups, or exacerbations followed by periods of remission. My journal entries tell especially of the exacerbations.

Now, twenty five years later, I have developed the secondary-progressive course of MS, which means the disease worsens more steadily. There are not so many flare-ups or remissions.

In my journal, I wrote about how MS was affecting my life, but I also had a lot of other things happening in my life during those years. The most important was raising my children. I was diagnosed with MS when my baby, Leah, was just a toddler. I am proud of the fact that I was able to raise my three kids from birth through maturity when they left home at eighteen. Of course, Rick was also there through the years. Thank God for that. My kids had to be very responsible from early on, probably more than other kids. Each one had specific chores to do. I remember Scott's job was to clean the bathrooms. One time, I got an empty Clorox bottle, cut the top out of it, and decorated it in a fancy way and put Scott's name on it. He was to use it to hold the cleaning supplies. Scott was not thrilled about his fancy, personalized toilet brush holder.

I am so proud of our children. All three of them graduated from Airport High School. Alan finished in 1986, Scott in 1990 and Leah in 1994. All of them also graduated from college. Alan is now married to Leslie. They met when they were both working in Savannah, Georgia and were married in Leslie's hometown of Quinby in Florence County, SC in 1992. They are now raising our two wonderful grandchildren, Meredith and Jenna, and live in North Carolina. Scott is now living in Philadelphia and Leah lives in Myrtle Beach.

During those growing up years, I did most of the cooking. I remember I had a high stool in the kitchen that I sat on to cook. Through the years, when I had exacerbations. friends from our church prepared our meals.

I was also a determined shopper. I had hand controls on my car and so I could still drive even after I lost the ability to walk. I would call K-mart before I left home and talk to the manager, explain to him my situation and tell him what I wanted to buy. He would meet me in front of K-Mart with the merchandise and I would pay him while sitting in my van. I did this with several other stores as well. People were very helpful. Eventually, I was unable to use the hand controls and had to stop driving all together.

A Typical Day in My Life

One of the things I wanted to include in my book was how I spend my days. When I started telling Mary Anne things I wanted her to write in 2003, this is how I spent most of my days. By this time, I had been having caregivers during the day for about three years.

A typical day begins about 7 AM in the mornings when Rick gets me out of bed. He puts my hose on me before he even gets me up. I can't get out of bed by myself anymore. He takes me directly to the bathroom. He leaves me on the commode and goes to work. He might bring me an apple or a banana for my breakfast. Then he leaves for work. I stay there until Shutong, my caregiver, comes around ten o'clock. During the 2 or 3 hours that I am sitting on the commode, I dress myself. I pick out what I am going to wear the night before, and leave the clothes next to the commode. I'll have to really be bad off for Rick to pick my clothes out for me. I might be wearing stripes and plaids together. I have a radio with a remote control to listen to if I want to, or not. Sometimes, I don't. I really value this private time to myself. I have had to give up so much of it, I enjoy what little privacy I have left. Often, I use this time to make phone calls. I have a group of people in my Sunday School class that I call every week. I usually call five people in my class each week. Occasionally, I fall asleep on the commode. I rest my forehead on the handrails installed beside me, and that's it.

When Shutong comes in, she puts me in my chair, and I wash my face, brush my teeth, and put on my make-up. This takes me until about 12:30. Then it is almost lunchtime. Shutong does everything I am not able to do. She prepares lunch, cleans up after lunch, cleans the house, and does the laundry. Her biggie is getting me on and off the potty.

Lunch with Shutong might last two hours. Often she wants to read to me. Sometimes we sit on the porch for lunch. We usually turn on the TV around 4 o'clock and watch some of Dr. Phil and Oprah. Around 4:45, Shutong takes me to the bathroom for a few minutes before she leaves at 5 PM. She gets me off the potty before she leaves unless Rick is going to be late. Then, she leaves me there until he comes in. But most days, he gets home about 6. If I do have to stay in the bathroom until he comes in, I have a little TV in there to watch. Scott gave it to me.

After Rick gets home, we have dinner. Around 7:30 or 8 o'clock, Rick helps me get ready for my shower. He takes my clothes off, places me in the shower, and gets the water the right temperature. I take hot showers cause they feel so good to me. I shower by myself; I'm a big girl. He comes to get me out of the shower and puts me on the toilet, where I sit for a while. He puts my gown on while I'm sitting there. After Rick gets me off the commode, I pick out my clothes for the next day, listen to the radio, or watch TV, or make phone calls. Rick goes to sleep before me, usually around 9 o'clock. I have to wake him to put me to bed, usually close to 11:30. He also puts my portable potty beside the bed.

Losing My Independence

As my condition worsened over the years, one of the most difficult challenges I have faced is losing my independence. In giving up that independence, I have also had to give up more of my privacy. This has been very hard for me. I am usually alone for a few hours each day, and I enjoy this private time. I hope I will be able to continue to have this private time alone for a long time.

I am also concerned about forgetting things. It seems to be happening more and more lately. The memory part of my brain has gone bananas.

What Keeps Me Going

There are several things that have kept me going during these difficult years. One of them is a quality I inherited from my Mother-that is determination. I have enough of my Mother in me to be a fighter, not to give up. She fought cancer several times. She also was determined to learn to drive a car, and even though she was 45 years old when she finally learned, she was determined to do it. Now, from my Daddy I got my temper. The Glenns were known for their temper. I've had one myself, although mine has cooled down over the years. My illness has taken away my temper.

I learned the value of hard work from both my parents. Mother and Daddy both worked hard all their lives. Daddy worked in the Duck Mill where the SC State Museum is now, and Mother worked in the Olympia Cotton Mill as a spinner or a spooler. Daddy was also a smart man. He realized the value of land and knew they weren't making any more of it, so he bought land for back taxes. That's how he was able to buy the property out here where we live now. He left land to all of his children, L.D., Betty, Nev and me.

48

But the single, most important influence in my life has been God. If I didn't have God in my life, I'd take a gun and put it straight to my head. It would be all over. It is only through God that I am able to get through my days. He has promised me that I will have a brand new body that will last me for the rest of eternity, and I believe that promise. That is what keeps me going. This body that I have now is like a tent. One day God is going to take this tent down and give me a new, perfect body. His promise gives me hope that I've got something better coming-that it is waiting for me in Heaven. That promise is in the Bible, II Corinthians, Chapter 5, verses 1-10.

1.For we know that when this tent we live in now is taken down, when we die and leave these bodies, we will have wonderful new bodies in heaven, homes that will be ours for evermore, made for us by God himself, and not by human hands.

2. How weary we grow of our present bodies. That is why we look forward eagerly to the day when we shall have heavenly bodies which we shall put on like new clothes.

3. For we shall not be merely spirits without bodies.

4. These earthly bodies make us groan and sigh, but we wouldn't like to think of dying and having no bodies at all. We want to slip into our new bodies so that these dying bodies will, as it were, be swallowed up by everlasting life.

5.This is what God has prepared for us and as a guarantee, he has given us his Holy Spirit.

6. Now we look forward with confidence to our heavenly bodies, realizing that every moment we spend in these earthly bodies is time spent away from our eternal home in heaven with Jesus.

7. We know these things are true by believing, not by seeing.

8. And we are not afraid, but are quite content to die, for then we will be at home with the Lord.

9. So our aim is to please him always in everything we do, whether we are here in this body or away from this body and with him in heaven.

10. For we must all stand before Christ to be judged and have our lives laid bare-before him. Each of us will receive whatever he deserves for the good or bad things he has done in his earthly body.
* from the Living Bible

More Changes

Late in 2003, I had a supra pubic catheter put into my bladder. In some ways, it was a good thing. It enabled Rick and me, especially Rick, to get an uninterrupted night's sleep. It also meant that I wouldn't have to be put on the potty so many times during the day. It allowed car trips without frequent stops. However, I hated it at first. It was uncomfortable, especially when I bent over in my chair. The tape that held the tube onto my leg irritated me, and it had to be alternated on each leg every day in the beginning. The urologist inserted the catheter in a surgical procedure while I was asleep. The second day, it stopped up. The Doctor had to insert it again in his office with local anesthesia. It took hours and was very painful. It stayed in this time for 6 weeks. It needs to be changed out every 6 or 7 weeks. Rick was trained to change it at home. Rick also takes the leg bag off every night and hooks me up to the bag at the side of the bed. Then every morning he reattaches the leg bag. I hate this leg bag and I hate the tube in my tummy, but I recognize the need for it. I also see the benefit of not having to go to the bathroom so often when I go out someplace, to church or to a restaurant, or a play. I still say this is a terrible way to live.

Another interesting result of the permanent catheter is that I am having a bit of difficulty adjusting to being in the chair all day instead of spending so much time on the commode. The things I used to do while on the potty for long periods of time, such as making my morning phone calls, are not coming to me as easily in the chair. I seem to go into staring mode, just staring at things and not accomplishing what I used to do while sitting in the bathroom. It is different being in the chair all day and it is something I am not used to, even though I am actually free to do more things.

Dark Days

In the early months of 2004, it seemed that my problems were multiplying. I still was not used to the catheter, and did not like it. But I also was having other problems. The shaking in my left hand was worse and that made eating more difficult. My right hand stopped working a year ago. Getting food to my mouth now is almost impossible. My hand shakes so badly that the food often falls off my spoon. It almost makes me want to give up eating, but I keep on hanging in there and trying. Sometimes I use a straw to "drink" my grits or cream of wheat or soup.

I am also concerned about my forgetfulness. I am gradually losing my short term memory, and it is very frustrating for me. I often can't remember what I had for breakfast or for dinner the night before. I think part of the reason for this is lack of stimulation in my daily life. I am confined to my home most days, and I mostly do the same things every day, things which are necessary for taking care of my condition. This tedious routine adds to the monotony and boredom. I think these conditions add to my memory loss.

I mourn the loss of my independence. I am frustrated at not having time alone, and it is especially frustrating not to be able to care for myself. It is very distressing when others have to do everything for me.

This has gotten to be more than I can handle- the way I have to live. I'm really feeling discouraged. I just have so many problems. I have a pressure sore on my bottom and I can't get any relief from it. I continuously try to lift my hips up from the chair to take the pressure off, but it doesn't really help. My heels hurt from the tight hose that I have to wear to keep my feet and legs from swelling. My knee hurts. I've lost the ability to grip with my right hand. I feel like a mechanical woman, not a human being. It's getting unbearable. I'm getting discouraged. I'm tired of it and ready for it to be over. I've put up with a lot, but it's getting so bad. I have to

51

rock constantly to get my weight off my bottom. The bag depresses me. When I look at it, it is so depressing- to know that my body is dependent on these artificial means. My voice is even getting weaker.

I just need to verbalize these thoughts. I know there is nothing anyone else can really do-I just need to talk about it.

It is only through God that I am able to get through each day. He gives me the strength to keep going and the courage to follow through each day, and get up the next day and do the same all over again. I could not do it by myself. I have no strength alone. But with God, I am powerful, mighty. I can handle it with God. I'm serving my time here, but it will be over, and God has promised me a new, perfect body. That is what keeps me going.

I pray every day for the Lord to take me. If it happens soon, don't be sad, because that is what I want. I want to be in my new, perfect body that God has promised me.

New Hope

Around this same time, when things seemed so dark for me, I got a note from my daughter in law, Leslie, thanking me for what I had meant to her. Leslie told me that I had been her mentor and her spiritual advisor for the past 12 years. I was so touched by the loving note. I appreciate her telling that I had influenced her spiritual life. I can only hope that I have been able to be an influence on other people's lives because even with the problems I have, I try very hard to keep a cheerful attitude and a smile. I call the members of my Sunday School Care group on a regular basis to check on them and give encouragement if needed and make sure each household is OK for that week.

Friends and Special People

During the course of writing this book, my friend Mary Anne visited with me regularly. Those visits were always enjoyable. Mary Anne and I have been friends for so long and are so comfortable with each other. It's nice to be able to talk to her about anything and about family and people we have both known all of our lives. Sometimes we would have lunch together, often on the sun porch. Sometimes we would wheel outside and look at the flowers in the yard. On rainy days, we would sit in the den and listen to the rain coming down on the roof. On dark dreary days, I made sure we had all the lights on to brighten the rooms. Sometimes we would listen to a CD. I loved listening to those funny old Ray Stevens songs or Floyd Cramer favorites from our teenage years.

We celebrated our 58th birthdays in the spring of 2004 and couldn't believe we were that old. My birthday is April 27 and hers is June 2, just a few weeks later. We talked about old times, as children and teenagers. We shared stories about our families and the things we did when we were young. We talked about our grown children and the joys and sorrows that go along with parenthood. I told stories of my wonderful grandchildren with much pride, naturally. I told her stories about people in my life that she didn't know, who for one reason or another came to mind.

One of those stories was about Al and Louise Driver. Sitting in my kitchen reminds me of them, because Al built the cabinets across the side of my kitchen. Al had such a creative mind and was also a good listener. Louise was the talker of the pair. What a card she was and a special person. I knew them in 1986 when I first went into a wheelchair. Louise tried to urge me to walk a little more instead of going into the chair. Louise had no idea how hard it was for me. I enjoyed those two friends. It was a joy to have them sit at my table.

Another unique character I remember is James Sturkie. James remodeled my kitchen and installed the beautiful front door on our home. He was an artist. He could take nothing and make something beautiful out of it. He would sit with me for an hour and tell me a story. He asked me once if I had friends who came to see me. I was touched by the concern in that question.

Yes, I have had many friends visit me. Over the years that I have not been able to do things in my home like cook and clean, Rick and I have been blessed with family and friends who have helped in so many ways. My older sister and friend, Betty Vining has always been there for me. She has cleaned my house many times when I couldn't and cooked for us as well. She took me shopping when she was still able to get me into the car. We both enjoyed those shopping trips. Having Betty living close by has been so reassuring for me at times when I have been alone and needed someone to come help me with something.

In addition to Betty, I've had other family members who have helped me and visited me. Rudolph, Betty's husband has helped Rick and me many times when he was able. Their adult children, Mike, Gene, and Tricia have visited me and cheered me on. Mike has assisted me several times when I needed him. My niece Pam visits and often brings her wonderful pound cake.

My cousin Janet visits and often brings meals with her. Janet and I go back many moons, back to high school days. We rode to school and back home together. Janet remembers a day when I was driving my old 1946 Ford that my Daddy bought for me. I hated that old car. Janet said we turned off Highway 215 to go to her house, and she clearly remembers going around the curve there on two wheels. Could I really have been going that fast?

I also enjoy visits from Janet's Mother, my Aunt Elaine. My other sister, Nev, and her husband Oscar, live in Florida, so I don't see them often, but we do talk on the phone. I have so many good memories of spending time with them during the summer at Jacksonville Beach, Florida.

I have called on another close neighbor, Leon Whitlock, who has been our tenant and great friend for 17 years in the old house that I grew up in and still own. I have called Leon in emergencies and he always came. Once I even asked him to empty my catheter bag on my leg. It had to be emptied. Even though I was embarrassed to ask him, he assured me that he would do anything to help me. Another time my right foot fell off my chair platform and I couldn't move my chair without injuring my foot. I called and Leon immediately came to my aid.

Our church friends from Trinity Baptist have been wonderful. They have prepared many meals over the years for Rick and me. Those meals are always appreciated, especially by Rick, who otherwise does all the cooking. Often, the person bringing the meal will stay and visit or stay and eat dinner with us. One time, Barb Lawson, stayed for two hours and visited. I especially appreciate it when people stay and visit because I know their time is valuable. Yet they are willing to give up their personal time for me and I am grateful for that.

A special friend, Judith Simpson, sets up the schedule for these dinners brought by church members and friends. Judith is one of the reasons that I keep my sanity. She visits often and occasionally brings her mother, Irene McCutchen, with her. Judith and I have been friends for a long time. There was a time when Judith was going through a difficult time in her own life, and I was there for her. Now that I am having a rough time, she is there for me. I treasure her visits and her friendship, and I especially enjoy her quick wit.

Another good friend who calls often and keeps me straight over the phone is Janice Mixon. Janice has also given me surprise birthday parties on two occasions, my 44th birthday and my 59th. The latest one was in her home and I know everyone had a good time by looking at the pictures.

A special new friend is Mary Kropiwnicki. I was really lucky when I met Mary. About two years ago, she and her husband, Ron, moved here and started going to our church. The first time I met Mary, she looked in my eyes and said, "What can I do for you? I want to help you. I will clean your floors, wash your windows. Just tell me what I can do." And she really meant it. That's the type of person Mary is. She is a truly caring and compassionate person who genuinely wants to do for others. She is such a special person and a wonderful Christian. She began a Bible study group in my home once a week for me and a few other friends. I am so grateful for her wonderful friendship. Mary has even stayed with me several times overnight when Rick had to go out of town and did whatever needed to be done. She gave me my nightly shot and changed my catheter bag to my night bag. She got me into bed and did what was necessary to get me going the next morning. What a good friend she has been.

I am thankful for my friends and the things they do for Rick and me. I feel blessed by their friendship and their visits.

My Special Blessings

My special blessings are my grandchildren. We have two beautiful granddaughters, Meredith and Jenna, and they call us Mimi and Big Daddy. Their parents, Alan and Leslie, make videotapes of them and send them to us to watch. How thoughtful of them to do such a loving thing. We have videotapes of Meredith's first day in first grade, and Jenna's first day of Kindergarten, and video of them in their cheerleading class and singing in church and many others. Leslie and Alan are wonderful parents.

They visit us whenever they can. They used to live in Valdosta, Georgia. Now they live in Cary, North Carolina. They can't visit often, but Rick and I love it when they can come. Once, when they were visiting, Jenna said to Rick, " Big Daddy, it looks like Mimi is the Queen and you are her slave." I thought that was so funny. Thankfully, so did Big Daddy. Where would we be without humor in our lives?

In addition to videotapes, Alan also sends us audiotapes. He has written several songs and recorded them. He sings and plays the synthesizer and piano. He wrote a song for Leslie when they got married called Sixty Years Ahead. Another was written when Meredith was born. He is very talented and has such sensitivity. Rick and I are proud of him, as we are all of our children.

Dog Stories

Rick and I used to have a dog whose name was Buddy. Years ago, I was getting food out of the refrigerator. I dropped the bowl and spilled spaghetti on the floor. I was having a hard time cleaning it up, when suddenly I realized I had a dog. I let Buddy in and he cleaned up the mess better that I could have. How simple life can be.

We got Tanner in 1997 when he was 6 weeks old. He is a wonderful Golden Lab and is very loyal. Sometimes I worry about Tanner. I think he gets depressed, but Rick disagrees. He doesn't think dogs get depressed. But I watch him in the yard and in his dog house and he sometimes looks sad to me.

One Saturday Rick was in the side yard working. Tanner came over to him, stood by him and barked. Then Tanner ran to the other side of the yard. He kept doing this, running to Rick, barking, then running to the other side of the yard. Rick tried to quiet him, telling him there was nothing there. Finally, Rick walked with him to the other side of the yard to see what Tanner was barking about. That's when he heard me calling him from inside. I had fallen out of my chair and had been calling him for help. My loyal Tanner was trying to alert Rick. We were both surprised and pleased with our "rescue" dog.

New Doctor

In September of 2004, Rick took me to see Dr. Mary Hughes at the MS Center in Augusta, Georgia. It had been eight years since I had been to a neurologist. This visit was mostly for an evaluation. I weighed 100 pounds, which I was pleased about. I felt like I weighed 20 pounds more than that. Some of the medicines I had been taking were no longer effective, and Dr. Hughes gradually changed my medications over the next few weeks. She also ordered a new chair for me, a chair designed to help with several problems I am having. One is my spine is beginning to curve because I can't sit up straight in a chair. The other is that pressure sore that causes me so much discomfort. The new chair is supposed to take some of the pressure off my bottom and let me sit in a more semi-reclining position. I will go see Dr. Hughes again in about a month. She said we would handle my issues one at a time. I liked her but she seemed very young. That may be because I am getting older.

Tough Days and Doubts

Some days are tough. Lord, I just read your Word from Proverbs 3: verses 5 and 6.

Trust in the Lord with all thine heart: and lean not unto thine own understanding. In all thy ways acknowledge him, and he shall direct thy paths."

I'm not trusting in anyone but You, God. With my body in the situation it's in right now, I'm not able to do anything for myself and others have to help me with everything. It makes me wonder sometime what purpose I can serve in this life. I can't do anything for anyone else, for a friend or a loved one. The only thing I can do is to cause them to have more work. It makes me wonder why God would leave a person on this earth under these conditions, unable to care for himself. Unless it is a test for those around them to see how well they will hold up or how strong they are.

I just know what Proverbs 3; verses 5 and 6 tell me, to trust in the Lord with all my heart, and that's what I'm doing. I'm not trusting in anyone but You, Lord.

If, in the end, if none of the Bible turns out to be true, if it is just a fake or a book of psychology, then what if I'm wrong. What have I lost? I have been a good person on this earth as a result of following the Bible. I have nothing to lose. But, I don't believe it is a book of psychology. I believe it is a book of truth, and at this point in my life, with my future being so bleak, if I didn't have the promises of the Bible to lean on I would have no hope, no hope whatsoever. Science, medicine, neither of these things has any hope for me. Maybe they're looking for a cure, maybe they will find one. But I can't imagine that happening in the next 100 years, if ever. So I just go step by step each day walking with You, Jesus and being sure that everything is going to be OK, that I will come out on the safe side, that this is not all there is, that there is more-a lot more. The best is yet to come."

More Challenges 2004

I've been in my new chair for about a week and I really don't like it. I can't get to the bathroom counter in it-it's too big. I realize it will be an adjustment that I must make to help relieve the problems I am having with my back and my pressure sore. There is no point in my complaining.

Just like there is no point in complaining about my new bi-focal glasses. I need to get used to them too. It just seems that there are so many frustrations to deal with. I want to be able to keep myself going, not having someone else doing everything for me. I have such a hard time getting food to my mouth. My left hand jerks wildly, back and forth, back and forth. If I am holding something, I have to lay it down or drop it. Usually I don't get to put it down, it just falls out of my hand. This morning Rick left me a piece of toast with jelly and a cup of French Vanilla for breakfast when he went to work. After thirty minutes I was able to get some of the French Vanilla through a straw. The toast is harder to get. Every time I try to pick it up, I get grape jelly splattered on my white top. I never was able to get any of the toast into my mouth.

Life is slow but I keep trying. I remember my Aunt Beulah had spastic hands. I wish now that I had helped her more. I know now that she needed help. I remember one day a long time ago when I was pulling out of my driveway to run errands in my busy day, she was on her way to my house to visit me. I told her that I had to go somewhere and she went back home. How I regret that. I wish I had said, "Come on, Aunt Beulah, get in the car and go with me." I should have given her more of my time.

Sometimes when I think about my problems, I get a little down. I also think how vulnerable I have been. It is a miracle that I haven't had all sorts of infections. In that way I have been lucky. I give God the praise and I always have to remember that He is my comfort and my refuge and I believe in his promises. I know that without God to walk with me through this life on a daily basis, I could not do it. How anybody tolerates a single day without God, I'll never know.

Alan called me recently and told me he was so proud of me, the way I always keep my faith in God even through the valleys of my life. He said I made his faith stronger and thanked me for it. That really made me feel good.

Pleasant Thoughts and Memories

Sunshine makes such a difference in my day. I love to sit in my chair and look out my front window. It is such a pleasure to watch the many birds that gather at the bird feeders that Rick has set up right outside the window. I have beautiful cardinals as well as many other kinds of birds. There is one bird in particular that is mean. If he is there, no other birds will come around.

Thinking about sunshine reminds me of something Susie Stevens once told me. Susie was a little Japanese lady who was married to Harvey. She has passed on now, but she was a friend in my Sunday School class. I was talking to her on the telephone one day. It was a dark and gloomy day and I remember she said, "You go and have sunshine in you heart." I try to remember that.

Looking at the flowers and trees when they bloom reminds me of my God who created this beautiful picture and this beautiful landscape. And I don't mind the rain, because I know how good the rain is for all the plants-the flowers and the grass. God's rain is so full of nutrients. It is so much better than watering with the hose or sprinkler. Just look at the plants along the interstate, how healthy they are. They get their water from God's rain, not man.

Another of my pleasures is a little song that I learned from Grannie Green. I have sung it many days and I change the words to fit the situation.

Today is Monday, today is Monday,

Monday, wash day,

Everybody happy,

I should say.

Today is Friday, today is Friday

End of week day,

Everybody happy,

I should say.

Today is Sunday, today is Sunday,

Sunday, church day,

Everybody happy,

I should say.

Grannie Green would be shocked that many years after her death I still find so many instances that come up for me to sing her song and remember her.

I am reminded of another pleasant memory every night when Rick gets me in the bed. I have a little blanket that Rick puts over my paralyzed arm to help keep it warm. It always stays so cold. It is especially comforting to me because it was my first child's receiving blanket. When I was pregnant with Alan, I decided to make a receiving blanket myself. I remember driving to the fabric shop and purchasing two yards of material. I brought it home, cut it out and sewed it together, leaving a 6inch area open. I turned it and threaded a needle and manually sewed up the hole. Then I crocheted around it. For some reason, I only crocheted two sides. I didn't do the ends. That 40 year old blanket has become a comforting blanket for me every night. Thank you, Alan Greenbean, for inspiring me even though you weren't yet born.

I look back and I am amazed at the creative things I was able to accomplish. I was a crafty person in those days. I did lots of cross-stitch, most of it for other people. Mary Anne tells me that I made her one for her office when she had her first counseling job, and that she still treasures it. It is on the wall in her kitchen. It says, "Those who bring sunshine into the lives of others cannot keep it from themselves." I also did a cross-stitch for my sister, Betty with her last name Vining on it. It is a masterpiece and to this day hangs in her den. I wish I had made one with our name, Green, on it so I could look at it today in my den.

I never did much of that cross-stitch work for myself. I wish I had taken the time to do more for myself. Then I would have more reminders to look at today.

Rick's Medical Scare

In February 2006 something happened to Rick that had both of us quite scared for a while. I am going to let this part of my story be in Rick's words since it happened to him.

It began when a big, black dot appeared in my field of vision. That dot changed to a short fuzzy piece of yarn floating in front of my field of vision. I went to my family doctor, Dr. Harris, and he referred me to an ophthalmologist who sent me to a retina specialist. Young Dr. Waldorf found a tear in my retina. He explained that fluids can get behind the tear and it gets larger and becomes a detached retina, a serious situation requiring serious surgery. He said he would repair it with a laser gun, which he did. He zapped my eye to repair the torn retina in my right eye.

I revisited him two weeks later and he wanted to check me again in two more weeks. At that visit, he looked into my eye for an eternity, actually about an hour. He said he wanted to refer me to an ocular oncologist. My immediate thought was cancer. Sure enough, he thought he had detected a tumor in my eye that could possibly be melanoma. He told me to go to my family doctor and get a liver scan and a chest x-ray. Both of those doctors conferred and decided to send me to Emory University. This was a kind of a scary moment. So a week and a half later, on April 3, 2006, I left on Monday to drive to Emory in Atlanta. I took Claude Graham, a member of my Sunday school class to Atlanta with me. We visited Emory where I met Dr. Aaburg. He is a professor in the teaching hospital at the University. He explained that I would be seeing six doctors. They x-rayed, did ultrasounds, all kinds of photos of the tumor. After about four or five hours, Dr. Aaburg said he was very confident, 99% sure that it was probably an old tumor. It had some white specks on it that indicated that it had been there for a very long time and it was his professional opinion that it was benign and nothing to worry about. However, he wants me to return in six months so they can re-examine the eye. If there is no change in the size and shape and look of the tumor, they will release me. So on October 4th, I will return to Emory. For now, we will wait and see.

This is Rick, over and out.

I am happy to say that when Rick went back to Emory, they did release him and he has not had any more problems with his eye. I know that the prayers that went up for him were answered.

Another Medical Story from Rick

This is March 15, 2006. This is Rick telling this story, since Janelle was asleep for most of it.

For the last several months Janelle has had crystals forming in her bladder. Those crystals feel just like sand out of a play box. After a week or two, the crystals completely stop up her catheter, the supra pubic catheter, which was inserted into her bladder about a year and a half ago. The doctor told her that these crystals that formed are the bladder's way of trying to fight off an invader, which is the catheter. But nevertheless, the doctor told us that he thought if he could clean all the little stones and sand out of her bladder, then the rednisone, which I insert into her bladder each night through her catheter, could possibly take care of any crystals forming in the future. So this morning at 5:30 AM, Janelle and I got up. We went to Lexington County Hospital at 6:15 and checked her in to Outpatient Surgery. After going through all the rigamaroll of filling out all the different forms and going through all the different interviews about insurance information and all that stuff, we got back to a holding area at about 7 o'clock, or a little after. I helped her change into a hospital gown and they wrapped her in some nice, warm blankets. The anesthesiologist came in, the nurse anesthetist came in and did a little puncture in her left arm and started the first nite-nite medicine. Janelle was very relaxed, was never scared. She and I talked and joked the whole time. Both of us were very relaxed. At 8 o'clock, the doctor showed up and told us what he was going to do. He would go into the bladder and look around for any crystals or stones that had formed and remove them. He talked to Janelle and me for about ten minutes. But she was already off on her little dope trip, so she missed out on that. She doesn't even remember him coming into the room. About 8:05 they took Janelle down to the operating room. At 9:30 the nurse came and told me the surgery had gone well. When the doctor came and talked to me, he brought with him into the conference room some photographs he had taken of the inside of Janelle's bladder through the cystoscope. He and I were both flabbergasted at the number of crystals that were in her bladder. The bladder was full of stones. It looked like the bottom of a creek bed full of little river stones. Some of them were as big as an inch and a half long. He went in and broke those stones up and cleaned her bladder completely out. Now the rednisone that she is on is supposed to keep any new ones from forming, hopefully. She recovered and about six hours later, we left to go home. Janelle was bright and cheery and alert, and felt well enough to go shopping. So we went and bought a washer and a dryer. That is the end of my report.

Ups and Downs

I have two motorized chairs that I use every day. One is the old one, the small Rascal that I can maneuver into the bathroom and get to the sink and wash my face and brush my teeth. The other is the larger, newer one that I don't like but must use most of the day because it is better for my back. I have a third one that stays in our van, which I use when we go away from home. Rick calls it my Sunday go to meeting chair.

One day I was in my Rascal. It has the tiller in front and the button that I push to make it go. The key was in the on position, but I was sitting still. I leaned forward to pull open the bottom drawer of a cabinet. When I leaned forward, the chair lunged forward. It happened so fast that I had no control and I was thrown out of my chair. Next thing I knew, I was sitting in the floor. From the next room, Rick heard the commotion and came running. He asked, "What happened? How did you get there?" I was startled. I couldn't answer him at first. I didn't know what had happened. I didn't know if I was hurt. He left me on the floor for about 10 or 15 minutes because he was afraid to move me. I was cold and very uncomfortable. I am used to sitting on fluffy, soft pillows, not a hard floor. My hiney isn't familiar with a hard texture like that floor. When he finally got me up and put me back in my Rascal, I thought I was OK. It wasn't until the next day that my right hip was black and blue, and my right thumb was very sore. It felt like it had been broken. My left foot was also sore, like it had been twisted. It's still a mystery how that accident happened. I'm sure a video of it would be entertaining. Plus, it would explain how I got the bruises and the soreness.

Another time I almost fell out of my chair was one afternoon when I was in the house alone. I was in my big chair this time and I leaned to the left to straighten the afghan. I got twisted into a position where I was hanging over the side of my chair. My back muscles are too weak for me to get myself back up from that position and it was a painful situation to be in. I had my phone in my lap so I called Rick. Except I must have dialed the wrong number, because I didn't recognize the person who answered. He said his name was Matt, and I said, "Matt, please don't hang up." Then I explained to Matt that I was in a wheelchair and had fallen. I asked him to call my husband and explain to him that I needed him to call my sister and get her to come and help me. Thank goodness he followed through with my request. It wasn't long before my sister, Betty, came in and rescued me. She pulled me up out of my slumped position and got me back firmly in the chair. I am thankful that Matt made the call. Not everyone would have done it. If I had had to wait till Rick came home at 6:30, I would really have been in bad shape.

My Caregivers

At some point, probably about eight years ago, I could no longer keep up the pace of keeping my house clean, cooking, washing clothes and all the necessities of life. I had to start hiring caregivers to keep my life in order. The first one I can remember was Nellie Foster. Nellie stayed with me until her grown children convinced her that she was too old to be working so hard, and that's when she quit.

Connie Crenshaw was next. She was a good one. We got along well and she was very pleasant to be around. Life was good with Connie until Rick told her that he was going to have to start filing Social Security on her. Connie wanted no part of that, so she left.

Crystal Fallow came next. Crystal was a neat young girl who left when she got married and went on with her life.

My next caregiver was Shu Tong Harrison. Shu Tong stayed with me for about two years. She came from China and spoke very little English, but she tried hard. I felt like her American mother since I had to teach her so much about living in this country. Due to transportation problems that developed, she was not able to come to my home any longer. I missed her, but God had someone else for me.

Janice Lawson became my new caregiver in May, 2004. What an answer to prayer she was. Not only was she skilled in the nursing techniques I needed, she was also a wonderful person to be with, and she brought a new joy into my life. She became my good friend and was eager to do anything she could to make my life better. She potted plants for me, polished my nails, exercised my legs, read the Bible with me and helped me order new clothes from catalogs. She told jokes and we laughed together. She listened and cried with me when it was the right thing to do. She cleaned our house and did the laundry. She wrote notes to help me remember things. I was truly blessed to have her in my life. She was also with me for about two years. Finally, she had to leave to be able to spend more time with her Mother, who was sick and needed more of her attention.

After that, Judith Graham and Kathy Draton worked for me for short periods of time. Jill Dotson is my current caregiver and we click very well together. She even goes shopping with me sometime. Jill is a great cook and makes dinner for Rick and me almost every night. She does a good job keeping my house clean. She exercises my legs and arms daily. We have fun together.

Some of my friends are also caregivers at times. Mary Kropiwnicki has stayed with me several times. Also Mary Anne Allread has spent nights with me when I needed someone. My sister, Betty, has been a faithful caregiver for me for many years. She has always been there for me. When she was able, she did a lot of my housework and lifted me and cooked for me. She isn't able to lift me any more, but she still cooks sometime and comes by often and does my nails for me every week. I am lucky to have a sister like her.

The one person who has been a constant and faithful caregiver to me is my husband. In all these years having to deal with this lifestyle, the most precious person to me has been Rick Green. My life would have had to shut down without Rick's support in getting me through this whole thing. Without him, I would have crashed in under the circumstances of losing it all. Without him, I couldn't have gotten dressed or gotten into the car to go off anywhere. What a champion he has been to get me through a situation that nobody on this earth wants to be caught in. I am grateful that my mother-in-law raised a loving and wonderful man. Without Rick and my most precious Heavenly Father, I could not make it. But with the two of them and my many other friends, here I am today, still standing tall.

A Typical Day Now

Things have changed since 2003 when I last described a typical day. I will give you readers a glimpse at what most of my days are like now in 2008.

Rick gets me awake about 6:30, disconnects the bag my catheter is hooked up to overnight and connects my leg bag which I wear all day. He puts me in my Rascal and starts dressing me. He stands me up and takes my pajama bottoms off and puts on my long pants that I wear for the day. Then he puts on my socks and shoes, then my shirt. Then I go in my Rascal to brush my teeth and wash my face. Rick then puts me into my big chair that I will be in for most of the day. I go to the kitchen to have my breakfast that Rick has already made for me. Usually I have oatmeal or grits, occasionally scrambled eggs and bacon. Rick usually leaves for work about 7:45. I stay by myself until my caregiver comes around 10. After Rick leaves, I go to my bathroom and clean my hands with a baby wipe. I can't reach the sink to turn on the water in my big chair. I put on a little make-up. I can't do this very well any more. I especially can't line my eyes. After that, I may talk on the phone for a while, to different people about different things. So things aren't as gloomy as they may seem. Often there is laughter in the conversations, sometime crying, but that is usually about someone else.

My caregiver arrives around ten. She begins working at cleaning house or doing laundry. We may start working on a project such as cleaning out a drawer. Later, she makes lunch and we eat about 12:30. Jill is very nifty at coming up with new and different things for lunch. I really enjoy salads, romaine lettuce or cottage cheese with pineapple.

When we are done with lunch around 1:30, Jill uses my new Hower Lift to put me in a recliner in the den. This gives me a chance to get out of my chair and have some new cushioning for my bottom. I stay in the recliner with my legs elevated until 3:45. At that time, Jill exercises my legs. She then lifts me with the lift and puts me back into my chair, and does exercises with my arms. These arm and leg exercises keep my limbs from getting stiff.

After Jill leaves at 4:00, I stay by myself until Rick gets home from work about 6 o'clock. I may watch TV, talk on the phone or read. If Rick has a meeting and is going to be late, Jill may feed me before she leaves or someone may bring food.

After Rick gets home and we have dinner, he puts me in the shower and puts my pajamas on. Then he puts me in my Rascal so I can get to the sink and brush my teeth. Rick gets my clothes ready for the next day and lays them out. Then he relaxes in his recliner and often falls asleep by 9 or 10. I am a night owl and stay up later. When I am ready to go to bed, I wake him in the den. He puts me to bed and we go to sleep.

A Treasured Gift

On my 60th birthday, my children got together and decided to write letters to tell me how they feel about their dear old Mom. They framed the letters in a large frame. It proudly hangs in my bedroom to this day. The letters are like poems and they are beautiful. I will always treasure this unique and wonderful gift. I am including a copy of them.

For Our Mom

4/27/06

"I was not flesh of your flesh, nor bone of your bone.
But still, miraculously I was your own.
I have never forgotten for a single minute,
I didn't grow under your heart, but in it."
I must have been the luckiest little girl on the planet to have been chosen to be your daughter. As I look back, I wonder... Did I remember to thank you for all the things you have done for me?

For all the times you took care of me when I was sick or brokenhearted?

For teaching me the value of hard work, good judgment, courage and honesty?

Have I thanked you for the simple things...the back rubs, the laughs we've shared? If I have forgotten to express my gratitude for any of these things, I want to thank you now... and I'm hoping that you've known all along how much I love you and appreciate you and how thankful I am that God chose you to be my Mom.

Love, Leah

This Earthly Tent Me, God and MS

I wanted to take time to express all of your worth,
It's not enough that you just gave me birth.

You've taught me so much in the life that you live,
You are truly someone who takes less than you give.

You possess a sunny outlook despite your condition
That makes us all stop before complaint is ever mentioned.

Many people share their struggles and problems with you,
They respect your opinion and the advice that you issue.

Your strong Christian faith is there for all to see.
It's been an example to others and truly to me.

I can't thank you enough for all of your love,
And for sharing that it all came from God above.

There surely aren't enough words here for me to express
How much you've meant in my life's success.

I love you, Mom.
Love, Scott

You are strong.

You boldly face challenges every day that most people never give a second thought.

Your fortitude in adversity has made me stronger.

You are humble.

You have empathy and understanding for things that many people will never face in their lifetime.

Your journey has made me more humble.

You are faithful.

Your unwavering walk with God has been a testimony and comfort for many, including your husband and children.

Your example has made me more faithful.

You are compassionate.

You take the time to care about people that many do not.

Your concern for others has made me more compassionate.

You are wise.

You have taught me to pray for wisdom and seek His guidance in all areas of my life.

Your discernment has made me wiser.

You are daring.

You step out and speak about the things that God says are important, regardless of what people say.

Your boldness and determined spirit have made me more daring.

You are thankful.

You give thanks for things both great and small and cherish the things that many people view as entitlement.

Your deep appreciation has made me more thankful.

I am grateful that you have shaped the course of my life through example in such a gentle and dramatic way.

Your family members and friends are better people because of who you are.

What a legacy, Mom.

I love you, Alan

Looking Ahead

Well, I have told my story. My life goes on. MS has taken control of most of my body, but my Spirit remains strong and my faith in God is forever.

I don't know what is ahead for me, but I am grateful for the time I have had and the love and support of my husband, my family and my friends. Most of all, I am grateful for my God, who has given me the strength and courage to get this far, and He will continue to be with me forever.

Multiple Sclerosis is a tough disease. It is unpredictable and takes away your independence and ability to care for yourself. But with Jesus Christ in my life, I have been able to deal with my disabilities and focus on helping others. I know that this earthly tent that I live in is being dismantled. In spite of this, I am making the best of my life with the loving care of my husband, my caregivers, my family and friends. I also know that when I no longer have use of this earthly tent, that I will have my new perfect body that God promised me in II Corinthians 5: verses 1-10. That is the scripture that gets me through life on a daily basis. My hope lies in what is beyond the burdens and temporary suffering of this world. I hope my readers, whether they are my children, my family or friends, or someone I don't know, will see how important it is to have God in their lives and come to realize that God can and will get them through anything they might encounter in their lives. God tells us in Philippians 4:13,

I CAN DO ALL THINGS THROUGH CHRIST WHICH STRENGTHENETH ME.

Janelle's Parents
Gene and Lizzie Glenn
Their younger years

Lizzie and Tyson

Janelle and her sister, Betty
1992

Janelle and Mary Ann
2005

Janelle and Mary Ann
1956

Janelle and Mary Ann
1954

Janelle and Rick
Our Wedding Day
12-04-64

Janelle and Rick
1975

Alan, Leah, Scott
1985

Janelle and Rick
Alan, Leah, Scott
1985

Janelle and Rick
1986

Janelle and Rick
1986

Men in Janelle's Life
Rick, Alan, Scott

Leah
1992

Alan and Leslie
Jenna and Meredith

Our beautiful

Grand Daughters

This Earthly Tent Me, God and MS

From row: Mary Kropiwnicki, Janelle, Irene McCutchen
Back row: Mary Anne Allread, Judith Simpson

Mary Kropiwnicki and Janelle

Janelle – 2007

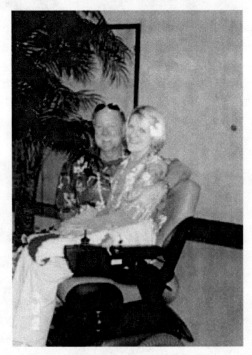

Janelle & Rick

Lora Switzer, Rick's Mom   Betty Vining   Janelle and Leah

Rick and his Mom, Lora

Tanner in the back yard

The following pages include letters and loving comments from Janelle's family and friends. She has touched so many lives and I want her to know what her life has meant to others.

Janelle, this is a tribute to you. I love you my friend,

Mary Ann

Rick Green

Janelle was the pretty blond in the new Mustang convertible in 1964. Wonder what got my eye…that stacked up Marge Simpson hair or that top-back Ford?

It really doesn't matter 'cause that was forty four years ago. If you ask today-it is the warm smile. She still has that gorgeous mouth and smile…it kills me. Did then-does now.

I met her in mid October and we got married December 4th the same year. Imagine that!

Janelle and I have always been able to "put on the dog" and appear as if everything is peaches and cream. Guess what? Everything is not what it appears. Although our marriage is sound, you really cannot "judge a book by looking at its cover." If only you could see the struggle of getting dressed, eating, putting on make-up (oh yes daily forever), or the simple task of counting change. I would give up my abilities to just share some with her. She is loosing it all, even her voice.

If you're feeling a little down by now, don't. Janelle would not have you spend even a moment feeling sorry for her, maybe me instead. You see, she really believes-all this life is short term.

She believes in her eternity in Heaven.

She believes that she will mount like an eagle and fly.

She believes she will run and not walk.

She believes in Jesus Christ as her Lord and Savior.

She believes a new body awaits her.

So do I.

Rick

Memories

Alan Green

I have many fond memories of my childhood, growing up in South Congaree. For me, many of the best memories involve my mother. As I was growing up, she would often do things to make me feel special. For instance, I remember a time when she took me and my brother to McDonalds to get french-fries and a coke. I was embarrassed to eat a peanut butter and jelly sandwich while we were there, but I sure did love the fries and playground. How could I have known at the time that money was tight and this was her small attempt to give me a treat and a playground. Later, she was the one who noticed that I could pick out tunes on a small air organ we had in our house. With that realization, she enrolled me in piano lessons and started a love of music that remains one of my greatest joys in life. I am forever grateful for her intuition on that matter.

Mom was diagnosed with multiple sclerosis when I was 8 years old. During that time, I vaguely recall a series of mysterious illnesses that would land my mother in bed for days on end. And then, as quickly as the symptoms came on, she was back and doing what she always did with us kids. It was only later that I noticed that with each exacerbation of the disease, her body would not perform as well as it had before. At least visibly, the disease started as a slight limp or weakness in her grip, eventually progressing to more obvious symptoms. For me, a child, those symptoms and limitations would go unrecognized until I reached middle school.

Today, I am a marketer with a large pharmaceutical company. I have been in various positions with my company for almost 15 years and have enjoyed it very much. Part of my fulfillment in the job has always been the satisfaction in knowing that my company helps not only patients battling various diseases, but also their families. As anyone knows who has had a family member with an illness, those individuals are not the only ones affected. The illness of a mother, father, sister or brother has ramifications for the entire family. Pharmaceutical research companies like mine, provide important help for patients as well as their families.

Looking back, I remember my Mom and Dad playing basketball with me shortly before her diagnosis so many years ago. She was never a very good shot, but she was out there actively playing with me. On occasion, for exercise, she would even jog around the circular driveway in our front yard. Those types of memories seem very distant these days as I sit here, a 40 year old man. Indeed, my wife even recalls that upon their first meeting in 1991, if assisted, Mom could walk very short distances. In our 1992 wedding pictures, she stands tall, Dad's hand sure and steady on her back. My own daughter's, now 9 and 11, have never seen their Mimi walk and are quite interested when they see pictures of her not in a wheelchair. That's all they have ever known and a walking Mimi seems foreign and difficult to comprehend.

Despite all of the difficulties in coping with MS, Mom and Dad raised 3 healthy children and now bask in the glow of grandchildren. Mom's example to me is a life of perseverance and faithfulness; a legacy that I am trying to pass on to my children. And through my job as an employee with a pharmaceutical company, perhaps the small role I play in patient health will have a positive impact on families who face illness. After all, most certainly there is an 8 year old child somewhere with a chronically ill parent, building memories that will be carried for a lifetime. Though never easy, my mother has always faced her challenges with faith, poise and determination. For me, that's the most meaningful of memories.

Leslie Hoke Green
(Daughter - In - Law)

On May 2, 1992, I married into a family that I did not know at the time would lead me on the path to my spiritual salvation. I grew up believing in God, yet not having a personal relationship with Him. After my marriage to Alan, I began to have conversations with Janelle that would lead me to become more and more curious to the life I could have, if I would ask for it and allow it. Sixteen years now into this married life of mine, I am still exploring a more personal relationship with my Savior. I am blessed to be a part of a family that encourages and inspires me.

Janelle asked me to write about what I do during my days, so here it is.... I am a stay-at-home mom to Meredith and Jenna, who are now 11 and 9. My days are really quite exciting, even though mundane! I recently started beginning my weekday with quiet Bible Study. Instead of sleeping in, which I so love to do, I get up with Alan around 6 a.m., go downstairs so that I may worship in private, before the day gets chaotic. It took me 40 years to get there, but I love it now that it's a part of my routine. This too, is another thing Janelle encourages me to do. She has, for as long as I've known her, had prayer time in the mornings.

Usually Mondays, Wednesdays and Fridays are workout at the gym days (I like to think it actually ends up that way *each* week, but unfortunately it doesn't). Tuesday is deep clean the house day then off to the school to tutor in Reading. We come immediately home from school to have piano lessons for both girls at our house. Wednesday is a pretty free day until after pick up at school. We then head down to church where the girls both participate in the choir programs.

I also have a group of girls that meet there to wait on our children. Sometimes we talk, sometimes we do a small Bible

95

Study. Thursday morning is a day where I meet with my small group at various homes or a café for our weekly Bible Study. EVERY day is laundry day. I still haven't figured out how my friends with 3 and 4 children are sane at all with this. Other activities slowly creep into my days. Things such as various PTA chores, field trips, parties in the girls' classes at school, play practices for school or church, birthday parties, etc. all take their various places in our schedules.

Most of the time, I appreciate being a stay-at-home mom. I know it's not a glamorous job, but it's the one we've chosen to keep our family more closely knitted together. The most encouragement I get is from my sweet mother-in-law. If ever I have a day when I doubt I'm in the right profession, I can call her for reassurance. What a blessing she is to all who have the pleasure of knowing her.

Memories

Meredith Hoke Green

(at age 11)

One of the many memories I have of my Mimi is when I was little she would always sing, "Meredith green bean I appreciate you." Too young to realize that Mimi was not her real name, I would sing back, "Mimi green bean how much I love you." Even to this day she sings that song.

As years went by I had made many more valuable memories. Sitting by Mimi's pool, going to the fair and many others. One of the people who has been a major influence in my life is definitely my Mimi. She has inspired me to love my Lord. She is always pushing me forward. She is a role model to everyone.

One of my most recent accomplishments is making the lead role in the school play and the church play. Mimi is going to come see the church one, and I can't wait. I take piano and voice lessons and was in the school choir program. If you think about it, Mimi inspired me to sing. (Mimi also loves to sing.) I don't know what I'd do without her.

Written by Meredith on March 27, 2008

Jenna Margaret Green
(at age 9)

These are some deep descriptions of my life and what Mimi means to me. I was born with a hole in my heart. I couldn't understand it but somehow I knew. When I was three I had to have heart surgery. It didn't even hurt!

I am an outdoors girl and I <u>LOVE</u> to eat <u>Chocolate</u>. I love to jump rope. It's <u>so</u> much fun. I also like to climb trees. I basically like to do anything outside. But sometimes I can just sit and read. Mimi can agree with that.

Have you noticed how I have been saying Mimi? Well, that's my grandmother. She has M.S. Her friend is typing this book. But I love Mimi and she loves me that's all that matters. But, that's what family does.

Written by Jenna on March 27, 2008

With Love, From Scott

You sometimes hear about the plight of the middle child in a family. Some experts feel that the middle child feels neglected in a household where the "baby" and "first-born" obtain certain privileges. I can truly say that my mom never let me experience this "middle-child syndrome." I feel she worked hard to secure my place in the family dynamic growing up. She was and is a fair, kind, and loving mother to both me and my siblings.

I'm thankful to my mother (besides giving birth to me, feeding me and providing shelter) for the memories of a pleasant childhood. There were comical moments like flying over the speed bumps at the airport in our Pinto station wagon or purchasing the "Lil Nibbler" for four of us at the Whale's Tail restaurant. There were experiences we shared as a family on trips to Washington, DC and Denver, Colorado. And then there are just everyday experiences I can remember with her as a stay-at-home mom. I'm glad her health was there when we were young, but early on there were signs of Multiple Sclerosis.

It has been difficult to watch the slow progression that MS has taken on her over the years. I remember when she first started to use a cane, but only occasionally. At one point she even purchased a combination cane/stool if she ever needed to take a rest. Next came the Canadian crutches, which I had only seen used by children on the Jerry Lewis telethon. She never got used to those crutches and the combo cane/stool proved to be too heavy to be practical. A push wheelchair was, at first, just used for long distances. I can recall her actually pushing me in that chair when I got hypoglycemic at Disney World. As the progression continued so did her need for an electric wheelchair. What she got was less a chair and more of a scooter.

"She was a little rascal on her little rascal" was the commercial slogan. As the disease continued she became more and more dependant on that wheelchair/scooter. I can remember when she was able to drive a car, even though that now seems so distant. At some point she had to have hand controls put on that Chevrolet Celebrity, but she was still able to drive us where we needed.

I thought the progression of MS had stopped or leveled off, at one point, when she stopped walking. I can see that it has continued now to the point where she has less and less use of her arms. The one thing the MS cannot take away from her is her positive spirit, her love and her faith. She is one of the finest individuals I have ever known. She has a strong Christian faith that has personally inspired me and many others. I'm sure that is the reason she remained so positive through everything: her faith in God.

Like many others who have a personal experience with a particular disease, I hope a cure is one day found for M.S. There are drugs that further slow MS's progression, but unfortunately mom could not tolerate these medications. I hope she is benefiting from modern medicine in some way, because she takes a fist-full of pills every day for something!

Despite her health condition through the years, I hope she knows that she has been a great role-model and mother. Someone should crown her "mother of the year." Wait a minute, I think she was the MS society's "mother of the year" in the 80s. Maybe "mother of the century" would be a more apt title.

Love from Leah

Janelle is my Mom. She became my Mom when she adopted me from Vietnam when I was just an infant. She and my Dad decided they wanted to help someone else less fortunate than them and bring her into their home and into their lives: a baby they didn't even know. Even though at this point, my Mom already knew she had MS, she still chose to give herself to someone that needed her. The older I get, the more I appreciate and love this about her.

She has taught me so much I cannot even begin to put into words. One of the many things she has taught me is that no matter how bad it gets, it can always get worse, so be thankful for what you have because there is always someone out there that has it worse. Her strength and faith is such an inspiration to me. It makes me so proud to hear others talk about my Mom and what she means to them as well. If ever there were an angel on Earth, I would definitely say my Mom has wings.

She has always loved and supported me through every point in my life, even though she may not have agreed with the choices I made. But I know this is because she would only want the BEST for me, ever.

I hope that when she reads this she knows how much I love and admire and respect and miss her. But I also hope that she already knew that, because not a day goes by that I don't think of her and hope she is safe and happy wherever she is.

Happy Birthday, Mommy. I love you so much!!! Thank you for everything you do and everything you are! I feel truly blessed that God chose you to be my Mom.

Thoughts from Mary Anne Allread

Helping Janelle write her book has been a labor of love. I am reminded of the saying about the most important part of a journey not being the destination, but the journey itself. I have been blessed all along this journey. We started talking about her book four years ago. Since then we have spent lots of time together. A lot of that time had very little to do with her book. During our visits and talks, we renewed our childhood friendship, reminisced about old times, caught up on the years we weren't in close contact, discussed our families, as well as religion, politics, and even Oprah. Janelle and I have known each other all of our lives. We were born about a month apart and lived very near each other for our whole childhood. We were close friends who played together, went to school together, and attended church together.

During our teenage years, we shared many joys and sorrows with each other as only teenagers can. Our friendship is an old one and that is often the most lasting and loyal kind. As we grew up and married, we didn't see each other often, but we still felt that same closeness whenever we did visit and talk. As I have typed from her journal and listened to her telling of the difficult times she has had, I regret that I did not see her more often over the years. I am sorry for all she has had to endure and still does each day.

I have learned a lot about MS and what it can do. But through Janelle, I have also seen what faith and courage and determination can do and how powerful these virtues are. Janelle's faith in God and His Word is unfaltering. Her determination is strong. She does not give up until she has to. Her strong will has enabled her to continue to do things for herself that are so difficult most of us would have given up much sooner. Her spirit is beautiful. She is cheerful and pleasant and does not complain about her situation. She wants to help others and makes many phone calls to give people encouragement.

She willingly tells others about her God and how he helps her get through each day. She is a true Christian and a living testimony of God's love. I am so grateful for the opportunity to help her write her book and have been so blessed by the experience. May God bless her and those who read her book.

More Thoughts from Mary Anne Allread

May God also bless Janelle's wonderful husband, Rick. Rick is a caring and compassionate man. He has been a constant, loyal and loving source of support for Janelle for all their years together. They have been married for forty- three years and MS has been a part of their lives for more than thirty of those years.

During that time, Rick has also been very successful in his sales career and has also been active in his church and civic groups. He is currently teaching a Sunday School class at Trinity Baptist Church and is involved in many other activities there. He has served on Town Council in South Congaree and also acted as a municipal judge for the town. He is an excellent and humorous public speaker and is often asked to emcee special events at his church and work.

He has been a good Father to his children and has enjoyed his role as "Big Daddy" to Meredith and Jenna. When his children were smaller, he even managed to have a successful side career as Tricky Ricky, a local magician who was quite entertaining. In addition to all this, he even finds the time to play an "occasional" game of golf. I've even been told that he plays a pretty good game.

He is also Janelle's most important caregiver. He takes care of many of her daily needs, including doing what has to be done to her catheter, giving her injections, and bathing and dressing her. He feeds her, cooks many of their meals, and even styles her hair and puts on her make-up when they go out. I have heard him tell her many times how beautiful she is. He is a special kind of man. He was given many talents, and in turn, he has given so much of himself to his sweet wife.

Rick, you are one of a kind and I am proud to be your friend.

This Earthly Tent Me, God and MS

If I were asked to describe my dear, precious friend Janelle, it would not be as a victim of MS. Instead it would be by her heart and her spirit.

First and foremost, she loves her Lord and Savior wholeheartedly and trusts Him completely. Even in the toughest of times in the thirty years I have known her, I have never once seen her faith waver.

How I admire her spirit in the midst of the many things she has had to endure. She always manages to break into that beautiful smile of hers and you see the Lord shining right through.

And talk about a CARD ministry! There are many, many people who have felt her care and concern for them through those wonderful cards she was so faithful to send. Call me a pack rat or a sentimental old fool, but I still have a stack of them that I was the most fortunate recipient of. Even though she is no longer able to write, she does not let that deter her from giving an encouraging word by way of the telephone.

I don't know if she or Rick really realize the tremendous witness their lives have been to countless people. Their faithful attendance at worship, their smiles and reaching out to others in spite of their own struggles, and most of all, their steadfast faith and devotion to God "through it all" have truly been an inspiration to many.

Speaking of Rick, I would like to express my admiration of him for the excellent care he has given to her for these many years. His love for her and his unwavering devotion to her have been something to behold! Way to go Rick! HANGETH THOU IN THERE!

Janelle, I love you like a sister and after all, we are sisters in Christ. Thank you for honoring me with your friendship. I appreciate you to the utmost.

Judith Simpson

Janelle

When I was asked to write something about Janelle I eagerly agreed, but I have struggled. How can I ever say what she really means to me? There are not enough words. As I attempt this, please know that it falls short of the admiration and respect I feel for her.

I'll never forget the first time I met Janelle Green. There she was with that great smile and that little tilt of the head that invites you in. I had no idea that a friendship had begun that day, a friendship from which I would draw great benefit. Over the course of the next two years, I would observe what it is like to walk and dance before the Lord, though bound by a wheelchair.

We began a Bible Study. Weekly we prayed, laughed, cried, and studied God's word. As we prayed, answers came. No matter how great or small our burden, we have learned: He is strong, able and pleased to allow us to commune with Him. At times I have stopped by Janelle's house to pray with her. Sometimes she would lay on the couch, and I would lay on the floor beside her. Together we poured out our souls to God, and reached up to Him. There, in that family room at the Green's house, I have experienced some of the most precious and intimate prayer fellowship that I have known this side of heaven.

Janelle has taught me many things as I have watched her life, a life filled with faith and joy and a wonderful ability to keep on laughing. This ability to laugh in the face of what some might view as adversity has been a source of inspiration to me.

One day as we arrived for Bible Study, one of her tubes was malfunctioning and she was not able to come into the family room for study and prayer. She suggested that everyone come to where she was for prayer. We all entered into the "throne room" so we could go together to the Throne Room. That day we received an abundance of God's blessings. What a difference attitude makes.

106

There is one quality about my dear Janelle that I admire most of all. It's the graciousness that exudes from her. There is no earthly explanation for this, only the deep, abiding presence of the Spirit of the Living God, and the grace that results from the hidden person of the heart being submissive to His sovereign will.

I know of few more effective testimonies than a life lived out in obedience to God. A paraphrase from the book of II Corinthians describes that which we observe in Janelle. It is but a by-product of obedience:

But this precious treasure—this light and power that now shines within us—is held in a perishable container, that is, in our weak bodies. Everyone can see that the glorious power within must be from God and is not our own.

I love you, Janelley. Thank you for allowing us to see His light and power.

Mary Kropiwnicki

Memories from Janet Walker

Janelle, we had so many good times growing up it's difficult to focus on a few, but I'll try. The madras blouses and wrap skirts Aunt Lizzie made were the best. The crease you made in my right Weejun because you thought it looked better. But the most fun was driving your Dad's 1949 Mercury. Remember it took both of us on the hill by the Carolina Coliseum, my feet on the clutch and brake and your foot on the gas. It's a miracle we made it. What about the day the brakes went out when we were turning off 302 right onto West Dunbar Road on two wheels...God sure was looking out for us.

Janelle, you are an inspiration to me. You are always positive and point out the best of every person. You always minister to others with sweet tunes and words of encouragement. You definitely do God's work. I thank God for every thought of you.

With love, your cousin,

Janet

Thoughts from Aunt Elaine

Janelle, I fondly remember the Friday night downtown shopping trips and dining on Eckerds's 29 cent fried chicken special. You and Jan thought I wouldn't know you had skipped school...Mother knows.

Janelle, after a visit with you I always leave feeling better than when I came.

With much love,

Aunt Elaine

Janelle,

I moved from Asheville, North Carolina to West Columbia due to a divorce. I came here with no hope of knowing what I would do for a job. I had no friends here and I was scared to death. But I did have family here and my faith was strong.

Within a week, the Lord brought us together. You have inspired me in so many ways. I have watched you struggle day by day yet you never give up. I see your devotion to Christ, our Lord and Savior, and your constant care for your family and friends, and the prayers you have prayed for them, even for those you never even knew. I watch you daily making your phone call to see how others are doing. Yet you sit in your wheel chair paralyzed in both legs and no use in one arm, but determined to dial the phone yourself. You are the most independent person I have ever known.

I have been blessed to have you in my life. You have made me a stronger person by knowing you. I have a Bible verse in my car held by a sticky note. You gave it to me one day when I was feeling a little discouraged.

"I can do all things through Christ who strengthens me." I will always think of you when I read it.

Thank you for being the best boss I ever had. May God bless you always as through Him you have blessed me.

Your caregiver and friend,

Jill Dotson

3-7-08

Janice Lawson

I worked as a caregiver for Janelle from May 2004 to September 2006. This job was easy but could also be challenging at times. Each day was pretty much routine and a job I felt like pretty much anyone could do. Janelle would remind me that everyone couldn't do what I did. There were times that Janelle or both of us could get into some unusual and hilarious situations.

We were put together for such a time as this. It was amazing how the timing and circumstances for this came together. I had just retired from a job of 31 years and took a class to get my Certified Nursing Assistant license to start a second career. The same week I finished my classes I received a call from Rick. We didn't know each other but a mutual friend told him about me. Janelle and I had been neighbors all my life and I had never even met her. I am so thankful for the opportunities afforded me by Janelle and Rick. My time with Janelle taught me not to take for granted my good health and physical abilities. I don't know what the future holds for me but if I ever have to struggle with disabilities I will always remember Janelle and her determination and positive attitude.

I was humbled and grew spiritually due to my time in the Green's household. We had daily Bible reading and prayer together. Janelle even opened her home up to weekly Bible studies. I don't know of anyone else who is more loved and has as many friends.

Thanks Janelle, Rick and Tanner for accepting me into your beautiful home and becoming my dear friends.

I love you my friend,

Janice Lawson

Evelyn Taylor

Janelle has such an inspiring story and we can all learn from it.

When I think of Janelle's witness, I remember various lines from the hymn written by Ira B. Wilson, "Make Me a Blessing":

Make me a blessing: out of my life may Jesus shine...make me a blessing to someone today. Give as 'twas given to you in your need...be to the helpless a helper indeed, unto your mission be true.

Make me a blessing to someone today.

Janelle has truly been a blessing to all who have known her since the beginning of her illness. Her faith and assurance of Christ's love has shown through her struggles and has helped all of us. She has a faithful heart for the Lord and her deeds of kindness to others have brought sunshine into their lives. How wonderful to think that when Janelle can walk again, it will be into the arms of her Savior.

My Bible Study Partner/Example

I was first introduced to Janelle Green in a Bible Study Group that met at Becky Jones home years ago in Edenwood. I remember that evening of Janelle telling us that she had MS but would cling to her faith in God to go through days ahead.

Since I kept children and could not get out, I had been doing a Bible Study over the telephone from some time with Susan Crabb (during the kids nap time) when Ken and Susan decided to go to the Mission Field (Aug. 1989). Susan suggested I try to find someone while she was away that could continue what she and I had been doing. Susan suggested I call Janelle Green knowing that she was at home and would maybe enjoy that company and studying a book of the Bible over the phone. I called Janelle and ask her if she would possibly consider it and to think and pray about it and get back to me. To my surprise, Janelle agreed and that began a long friendship and time of studying the Bible over the phone. Sometimes we felt we knew each other much better over the phone than in person.

Besides studying the Bible, we started memorizing bible verses. I remember the very first verse Janelle suggested for us to learn together, Proverbs 3:5&6. "Trust in the Lord with all your heart, and lean not on your own understanding, acknowledge Him in all your ways and He will make your paths straight". I remember looking at those verses and thinking I will never begin to remember all of that. Janelle came up with all kinds of ways to help remember by pointing at our heart or using our fingers. That was just the beginning of our learning verses together. I still have an index card on my refrigerator today that Janelle wrote out for us to learn together. It's a little faded but aren't we all.

The only thing that does not fade is God love.

We lifted each other up through the ups and downs of our lives. Janelle could always fill in the silent moments on the phone when lumps came in my throat and I couldn't get a word out. God brought just the right person in my life and what a wonderful example He provided for me.

I enjoyed giving Janelle a couple of surprise birthday parties. Janelle's smile always filled the room. Janelle's sense of humor has always helped to get her through days that others would have found depressing.

Our annual looking at Christmas lights in December was always a highlight.

I thank God for bringing Janelle into my pathway.

I love you Janelle.

Janice Mixon   April 2008

MY FRIEND JANELLE

I have known Janelle and Rick and family since 1975.They have been such wonderful friends throughout the 38 following years, although there have been long stretches of time when we have not seen each other or communicated. They have always been a source of inspiration to me, particularly the early years of my becoming a Christian. Their witness and care for others has been so evident to all those around them.

I want to thank you, Janelle for encouraging me, praying for me and loving and caring about me all these years. I vividly remember 2 things. One was the day I stood in front of a Ladies Bible Study and asked them to pray for you as you had just been diagnosed with MS. I could barely talk through my tears. It struck me so profoundly. The other time was when you by faith asked the elders of the church to lay hands on you and anoint you with oil to ask God for healing for a type of cancer that you had been diagnosed with. God healed you of that but not your MS. I believe He wanted you here to be such a wonderful witness to all those you have been around since.

I think of you often. I laugh a lot when I think of you and Rick. You have brought much joy into my life and all of our family. I love you and Rick dearly. God bless you and your family richly. I know he has blessed us by letting us be your friends.

Love always,

Becky Jones

Janelle and Rick,

When we moved to Columbia in 1975, we were lost and lonely; yet, in just a few months, God connected us with some of the dearest people we have ever known: the McIlwains, the Joneses, the Crabbs, the Hucks, and, of course, the Greens! God seemed to knit our group together through church, children and a common desire to know and follow Him. Acquaintances rapidly became close personal relationships as we learned how to love and encourage one another. Those relationships enabled us to feel at home in our new environment and met our deep need for fellowship.

We were growing together in Christ in a church share group during the time you were seeking medical answers to some issues Janelle was struggling with. Our small group prayed fervently, and when the diagnosis of MS came, it was devastating. We didn't know all that it meant, but we knew it was hurting those we loved, and we hated it! We watched as you put your trust in the Lord and courageously walked the path He'd set before you.

In 1984, we moved away from Columbia, but whenever we return, the relationships we established there are like glowing embers whose fire is quickly rekindled. The few visits we've enjoyed with you have been so special as we've shared things we remember and tried to catch up on all that's happened. Mutual friends tell us how difficult things are for you, but we've seen first-hand how you've fought the battle with strength and grace. We've always left your presence inspired and thankful for the blessing we've received.

116

Rick, thank you for your commitment and love for Janelle! Within that Ronald McDonald costume beats the heart of a courageous man who has loved his wife as God intended: deeply, unconditionally, and sacrificially. Bless you for giving friends and family this powerful example of manhood. Janelle, we will always remember the beautiful lady you are—beautiful on the outside, but even more so on the inside, as your heart and mind reveal. May God continue to bless you both in every way; we're forever grateful that He brought you into our lives.

With love and admiration,

Audrey and Jim Laird

My Sister Janelle
By Betty Vining

My sister was born April 27, 1946. Janelle was born in our home. I remember the day the doctor came to deliver her. The doctor ordered us to boil his instruments on our wood stove. Daddy was in the bedroom with the doctor. When Dad came out, he said it was a boy. Come to find out he was just joking. It was my new little sister. After my stepmother went back to work, I had Janelle all to myself. I changed diapers and cared for her daily. I was fifteen when she was born, so Janelle did go with me on a few dates. She was a good baby and I enjoyed taking care of her. We spent a lot of time at home. I kept little Janelle while Dad and stepmom worked in the garden. I look back to that time now and I have no regrets.

When Janelle turned four I went to work. Three years later I married. After I married Rudolph Vining, Janelle came to visit me on occasion. We maintained our relationship over the years while my husband served in the Air Force. Rudolph and I retired here in South Carolina in 1974.

I have enjoyed Janelle the last thirty-three years. I admire her and how she has handled her MS. I have seen her start with small symptoms and progress to her present state. I took care of my little sister years ago. I love her and I am here for her again, just like years ago. I know she struggles each day and my little sister is always on my mind.

During our journey here on earth,

The people that pass our way are not by coincidence.

They are divinely there to increase

Our knowledge and understanding.

Some for direction, some for life lessons, and

Some for our joy and pleasure.

Some are remembered only for the moment

And then there are those that make a

Small indention on our hearts to be remembered

Always.

By Vanda Hucks

Janelle,

You are for direction, life lessons and my joy and pleasure.

You are one of the small indention on my heart.

This Earthly Tent Me, God and MS

This Earthly Tent Me, God and MS

This Earthly Tent Me, God and MS

This Earthly Tent Me, God and MS

Printed in the United States
133376LV00003B/40/P

9 781607 911548